TOPICS TODAY

The Marijuana Legalization Debate

By Kate Mikoley

Cavendish Square
New York

Published in 2022 by Cavendish Square Publishing, LLC
29 E. 21st Street New York, NY 10010

Copyright © 2022 by Cavendish Square Publishing, LLC

First Edition

No part of this publication may be reproduced, stored in a retrieval system, or transmitted in any form or by any means—electronic, mechanical, photocopying, recording, or otherwise—without the prior permission of the copyright owner. Request for permission should be addressed to Permissions, Cavendish Square Publishing, 29 E. 21st Street New York, NY 10010. Tel (877) 980-4450; fax (877) 980-4454.

Website: cavendishsq.com

This publication represents the opinions and views of the author based on his or her personal experience, knowledge, and research. The information in this book serves as a general guide only. The author and publisher have used their best efforts in preparing this book and disclaim liability rising directly or indirectly from the use and application of this book.

Portions of this work were originally authored by Hal Marcovitz and published as *Marijuana* (*Drug Education Library*). All new material this edition authored by Kate Mikoley.

All websites were available and accurate when this book was sent to press.

Library of Congress Cataloging-in-Publication Data

Names: Mikoley, Kate, author.
Title: The marijuana legalization debate / Kate Mikoley.
Description: New York : Cavendish Square Publishing, [2022] | Series: Topics today | Includes bibliographical references and index.
Identifiers: LCCN 2021010179 | ISBN 9781502661081 (library binding) | ISBN 9781502661074 (paperback) | ISBN 9781502661098 (ebook)
Subjects: LCSH: Marijuana–Law and legislation–United States–Juvenile literature. | Drug legalization–United States–Juvenile literature.
Classification: LCC KF3891.M2 M53 2022 | DDC 344.7305/4–dc23
LC record available at https://lccn.loc.gov/2021010179

Editor: Kate Mikoley
Copyeditor: Nicole Horning
Designer: Deanna Paternostro

Some of the images in this book illustrate individuals who are models. The depictions do not imply actual situations or events.

CPSIA compliance information: Batch #CS22CSQ: For further information contact Cavendish Square Publishing LLC, New York, New York, at 1-877-980-4450.

Printed in the United States of America

Find us on

CONTENTS

Introduction Cannabis Culture	5
Chapter One Cannabis Through Time	9
Chapter Two Cannabis's Impact on the Body	27
Chapter Three Cannabis Today	43
Chapter Four Medical Uses	57
Chapter Five The Future of Legalization	73
Getting Involved	90
Notes	91
For More Information	94
Index	98
Photo Credits	103
About the Author	104

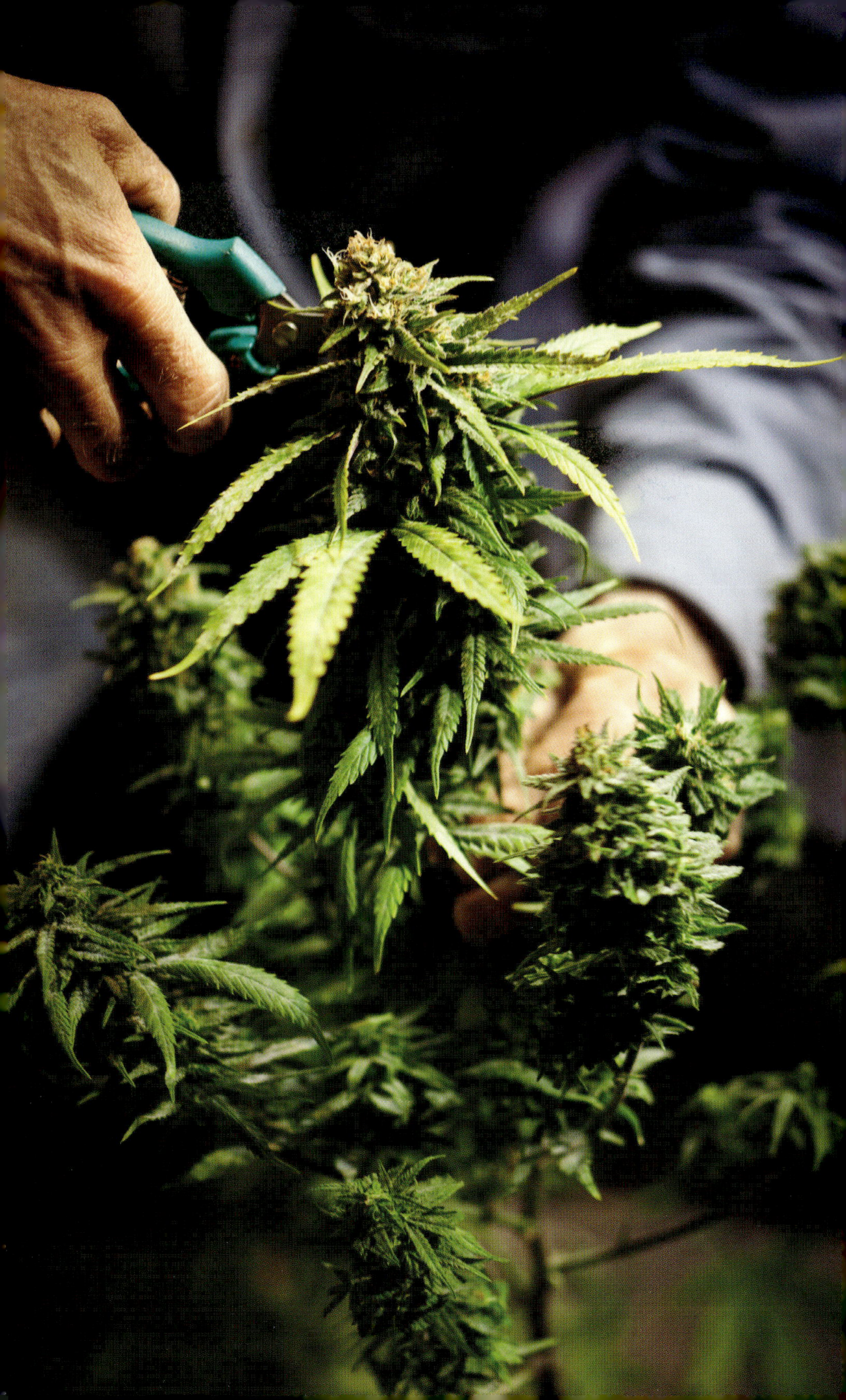

CANNABIS CULTURE

M arijuana is a drug known by many names, such as pot and weed. It is made up of dried parts of *Cannabis* plants. In fact, many people prefer to use the word "cannabis" when referring to the drug, as well as the plant. Technically, the word "marijuana" refers to products that come from the plant that contain substantial amounts of tetrahydrocannabinol (THC), while "cannabis" refers to all products that come from *Cannabis* plants. THC is the substance in the drug that is known to be primarily responsible for affecting a person's mental state, or getting a person "high." Studies have also shown it can also be useful in helping relieve certain medical concerns, such as nausea or vomiting that result from some cancer-treating drugs.

The word "marijuana" comes from a Mexican word used to describe the drug. Some people avoid using this word because of racist connotations. Many argue that the word was used by the U.S. government to provoke anti-Mexican and anti-immigrant feelings and therefore has no place in today's language. However, others argue that not using the word actually erases Mexican immigrants' influence on culture in the United States. In this book, both words may sometimes be used, particularly for clarification about different cannabis products and laws that use the word "marijuana." Unless it is specified to be referring to the plant, the word "cannabis" will refer to the drug (marijuana).

◀ Harvesting *Cannabis* plants to be used as drugs is nothing new. The plant is believed to have been used in ancient Chinese medicine to treat pain and other maladies at least as far back as 2700 BCE.

Is It Legal?

According to the National Institute on Drug Abuse (NIDA), cannabis is "the most commonly used illicit substance."[1] However, it's not illegal everywhere. In a few countries, it is legal for adults to buy and use recreationally. In even more countries, it is legal to use for medicinal purposes only. However, as of January 2021, cannabis is still illegal in most countries around the world. That doesn't mean, however, that the laws are always strictly or fairly enforced. In many places, cannabis use has been decriminalized. This means even though it is still technically illegal, police may not treat it as a crime, or they may not treat it as seriously as the law says to treat it.

In the United States, as of January 2021, cannabis is illegal on a federal level. However, the majority of the states within the country have legalized the substance on some level, whether it is for both medical and recreational use or solely for medical use. Even in states where it is only legal for medical use, it is often decriminalized for people found to be using it recreationally. Since cannabis is now legal in many states but has not been legalized federally, the issue can be confusing.

Cannabis legalization is a hot-button issue in the United States as well as around the world. Those who support legalization compare anti-cannabis laws to Prohibition, the failed attempt to outlaw alcohol in the United States in the 1920s and early 1930s. From the start, the law was unpopular and widely violated. By the time Prohibition was finally repealed, or revoked, in 1933, few people could say it had served much of a purpose.

Some people oppose cannabis legalization for recreational purposes but do believe the medical benefits are valuable. These people may support the use of the drug as a treatment for serious pain and conditions such as glaucoma or epilepsy. Others believe cannabis should not be legal for any purpose. They often point to the numerous health consequences that have been attributed to the drug—such as lung damage and loss of short-term memory—and argue strongly against any effort to legalize the drug.

However, researchers are still studying both the positive and negative effects of cannabis. While we know more about the drug now than ever before, there is still much to be learned and understood.

Many people have a picture of what they think a "typical" pot smoker looks like. However, there is no such thing as a "typical" pot smoker or cannabis user. People who use the drug come from all walks of life. In fact, around half of all adults in the United States admit to having used cannabis at least once in their lives. Additionally, according to a 2019 survey from the Pew Research Center, 59 percent of U.S. adults think the drug should be legal for medical and recreational use, while 32 percent said it should be legal for just medical use. Only 8 percent of those surveyed thought it should be illegal in all cases.

Where Does It Come From?

Cannabis is both grown in and illegally imported to the United States. It is produced both legally and illegally in states across the country. It is also smuggled across the borders from both Mexico and Canada. Some of it is even brought across the ocean to unlawfully enter the United States. Due to the illegality of the drug, it is close to impossible to find accurate statistics on the rates of production and importation of cannabis in the United States.

Some people point to finances as a reason why they think the drug should be legalized federally in the United States. If it is legal, the government can tax the drug. Additionally, it is possible more jobs could be created with the opening of dispensaries and production plants, which could benefit the economy as a whole. Even in states where cannabis is legal, growers are unable to ship their products to other states or countries, meaning they don't have the opportunity to make money exporting the drug. For example, Canada, which has legalized cannabis, was estimated to have made nearly $15 billion in the global marijuana trade in 2019. Many people say legalizing the production, selling, and exportation of cannabis could provide income to the United States. Still, others think the negatives outweigh the positives when it comes to the legalization of cannabis.

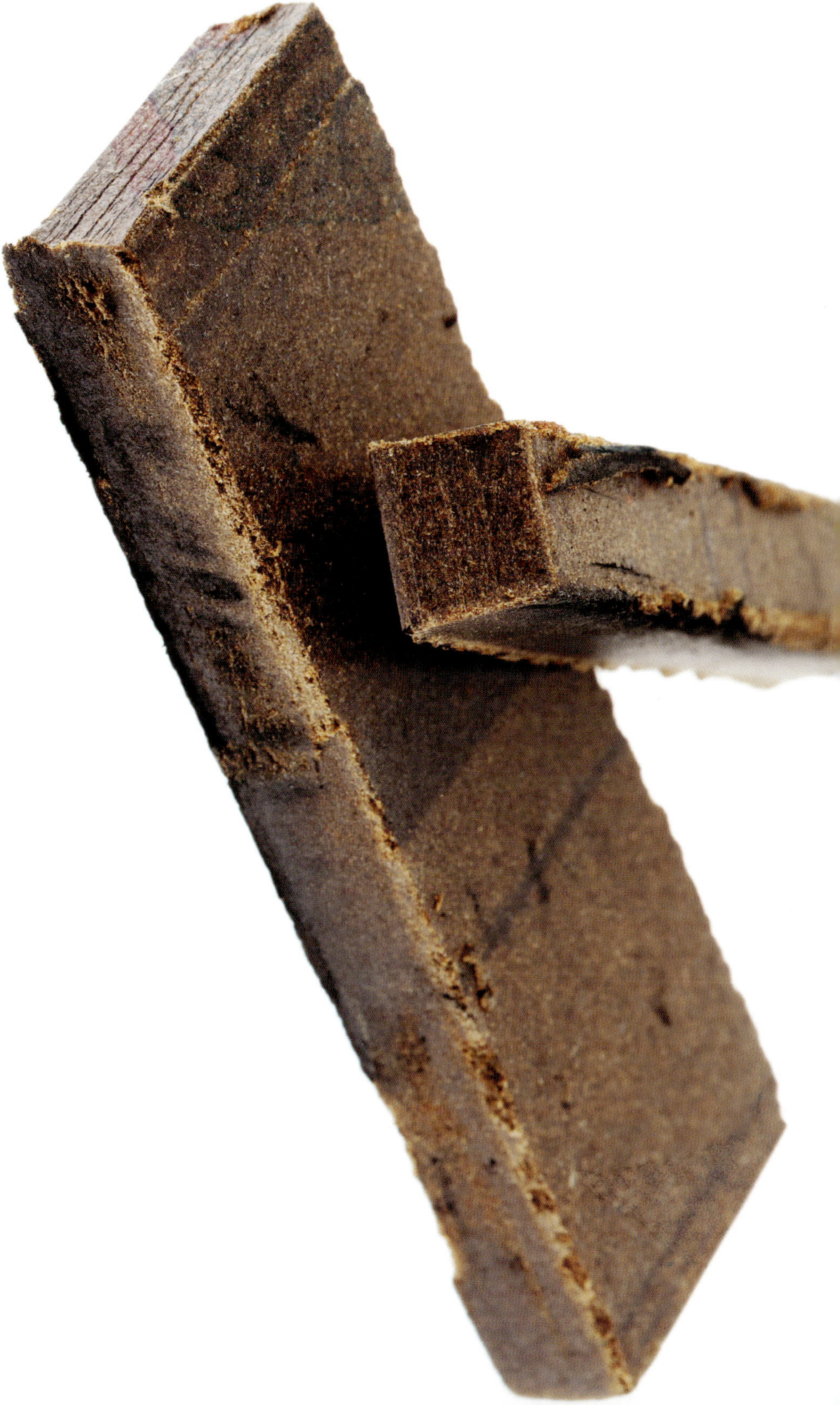

CHAPTER ONE
CANNABIS THROUGH TIME

Cannabis use dates back for thousands of years. The earliest known written accounts come from ancient China. Even when not mentioned directly, some ancient texts refer to drugs historians believe to be cannabis. At least one Egyptian mummy from nearly 3,000 years ago was even found to have traces of THC in its body. However, historians believe most ancient cultures did not grow the plant to get high, as it is often used today. Instead, it was grown primarily to be used as an herbal medicine, or a medical treatment made from plants.

Throughout history, cannabis has been used in many different ways, including as an anesthetic (a drug that reduces sensitivity to pain) often given before medical procedures and as an antibiotic. It has also been used to help people sleep, lessen pain, and lessen feelings of depression. In addition to being smoked, it has been used as an ointment that people could rub on their skin. In the 1800s, it was sometimes used internally to treat conditions such as chest pain and a sexually transmitted infection called gonorrhea.

◀ Cannabis comes in many forms, including bricks of hashish, such as the ones shown here.

Plant Terms

Technically, "marijuana" only refers to a drug made from the flowers and leafy parts of a *Cannabis* plant. However, for legal purposes, "marijuana" often refers to the entire plant. THC is found in the flowers and leaves of the plant but not in the stalk, which is the fibrous portion of a *Cannabis* plant.

Resin can be extracted from the plant and is rich in THC. When compressed into a paste, the resin is known as hashish or hash. One dose of hashish, which is typically smoked in a pipe, is said to have five to eight times the potency of a cannabis cigarette, commonly known as a joint.

There are two main types of *Cannabis* plants. The kind commonly known as marijuana contains THC and other compounds that, when smoked, give the user a high. The other kind is known as hemp, although both types of *Cannabis* are forms of the hemp plant. Hemp contains almost no THC and has many industrial uses. For a long time, both were considered Schedule I drugs, which the U.S. Drug Enforcement Administration (DEA) defines as "drugs with no currently accepted medical use and a high potential for abuse."[1] However, in recent years, hemp has been removed from this list. Other Schedule I drugs include heroin, LSD, and ecstasy. There can be high penalties for being caught using, selling, or transporting these drugs.

In addition to the two main types of *Cannabis* plants, there are two strains of marijuana called sativa and indica. They have different ratios of THC to cannabidiol (CBD), which produces different effects on the mind and body. Sativas are higher in THC than CBD, making the user feel "high"—thoughts race and the body feels energized. Indicas are the opposite, producing a "stoned" feeling—sleepy and numb, with slowed-down thought processes. For medical use, sativas are more commonly chosen to stimulate hunger in chemotherapy or AIDS patients, while indicas are used to relieve pain, muscle spasms, and insomnia.

Cannabis Comes to America

In the 1200s, Marco Polo wrote about an Arab prince who gave cannabis to his guards to enhance their courage. Other explorers who visited Asia and the Middle East brought the plant back with them, introducing cannabis to the European countries. Cannabis became a valuable crop, both as hemp and marijuana. European writers were particularly enthusiastic about cannabis; in 1844, some of the top authors in Paris, France—including Victor Hugo, Honoré de Balzac, and Alexandre Dumas—established *Le Club des Hashischins*, where they could share their hashish while pursuing their creative interests.

Cannabis arrived in America with the Jamestown, Virginia, settlers in 1607. The settlers grew the plant because they needed hemp to make their own clothes since supply ships from Europe rarely made their way to the colony. In fact, the hemp crop was so valuable that colonial governments eventually ordered farmers to grow it, fining them if they didn't comply. Evidence suggests that while the colonial hemp farmers did know cannabis could also produce a narcotic effect, few of them were known to use the plant for that purpose. For example, hemp was grown on George Washington's Virginia farm. Washington's diary entries report that he destroyed the leafy parts of the plant, causing historians to conclude that the Founding Father had no interest in consuming or smoking his crop.

By the 1800s, many Americans were legally using cannabis for recreational purposes. It was occasionally smoked, but at the time, most cannabis users achieved their highs by chewing and even eating the leaves. The more prosperous users could afford to visit secret hash parlors, where they smoked hashish in elaborate Arabian pipes known as hookahs that filtered the harsh smoke through water. These pipes have become popular again in recent years, but hookah bars in the United States today only offer their customers tobacco. In 1883, Dr. H. H. Kane described his experience in a New York City hash den to the readers of *Harper's New Monthly Magazine*. The hash smokers, he wrote, "are about evenly divided between Americans and foreigners; indeed, the place is

CBD

Even if you live somewhere where marijuana is illegal, chances are, you've seen a store with a sign saying they sell CBD products. If CBD and marijuana come from the same plant, why is CBD often not illegal in places where marijuana is? After THC, CBD is the second-most prevalent active ingredient in cannabis. CBD is present in both medical and recreational cannabis.

Today, CBD is sold in many forms. It is often sold in the form of an oil. Users apply drops of the oil under their tongue. Oils are sold with different potencies of CBD, so the amount in one dose differs from oil to oil.

kept by a Greek, who has invested a great deal of money in it. All the visitors, both male and female, are of the better classes, and absolute secrecy is the rule. The house has been opened about two years, I believe, and the number of regular habitués [visitors] is daily on the increase."[2]

Today, CBD is even available for pets. Some say it can help alleviate joint pain and reduce anxiety, but a person should always ask their vet before giving their pet CBD.

However, alone, CBD will not get a person high.

CBD is commonly derived from the hemp plant, a variety of *Cannabis sativa*. The hemp plant has many uses, such as for making fabrics and building materials. However, it only has a small amount of THC—not enough to give a person the "high" feeling. In fact, legally, hemp can only contain up to 0.3 percent THC. In the United States, cannabis plants with THC rates higher than 0.3 percent are legally classified as marijuana. Hemp does, however, contain high amounts of CBD. CBD is often used to treat conditions such as anxiety and pain; however, the full extent of its effectiveness is still being studied. All states in the United States have laws about CBD to some extent. Some states have certain restrictions, such as requiring a prescription. Additionally, CBD coming from plants with more than 0.3 percent THC is federally illegal in the United States.

At the time, marijuana and hashish were not illegal drugs in America. Although the rise of the cotton industry in the 1800s had made hemp a much less important fabric, cannabis was still widely grown on farm fields throughout the country. In fact, in 1914, Congress passed the Harrison Narcotic Act, outlawing the use of most drugs for recreational purposes. Cannabis was omitted from the law at the request of the hemp farmers.

The War on Weed

Despite its legality and perceived medical benefits, there was widespread belief among many leaders of American society and government that cannabis caused trouble. In 1913, California became the first state to outlaw recreational use of cannabis. Wyoming followed in 1915. By 1937, all but 2 of the 48 states in the country at the time had passed laws banning the drug.

In most cases, the state legislatures were prompted to act after newspapers reported sensational crime stories in which the perpetrators admitted to being high on cannabis. Stories such as this one from Universal News Service were typical of the time:

> *Shocking crimes of violence are increasing. Murders, slaughterings, cruel mutilations, maimings, done in cold blood, as if some hideous monster was amok in the land.*
>
> *Alarmed Federal and State authorities attribute much of this violence to the "killer drug."*
>
> *That's what experts call marihuana [marijuana]. It is another name for hashish. It's a derivative of Indian hemp, a roadside weed in almost every State of the Union …*
>
> *Those addicted to marihuana, after an early feeling of exhilaration, soon lose all restraints, all inhibitions. They become bestial demoniacs, filled with the mad lust to kill.*[3]

Today, a story such as this one would seem ridiculous to most people. While some studies have linked cannabis use to anger, others have suggested it actually reduces aggression. Like any drug, cannabis can certainly have negative side effects, and there are true stories of cannabis causing people to act violently toward others or harm themselves. However, recent studies suggest these instances tend to be uncommon.

In 1927, a campaign by newspapers in New Orleans prompted the Louisiana legislature to outlaw marijuana. Within days of the law's adoption, a New Orleans newspaper reported a wholesale arrest of more than 150 people:

> Approximately one hundred underworld dives, soft-drink establishments, night clubs, grocery stores, and private homes were searched in the police raids. Addicts, hardened criminals, gangsters, women of the streets, sailors of all nationalities, bootleggers, boys and girls—many flashily dressed in silks and furs, others in working clothes—all were rounded up in the net.[4]

Other states began to ban the drug as well. However, at this time, using or selling cannabis was still not a federal crime. In this way, it was the opposite of how it is now, where many states have legalized it, but the federal government still recognizes it as illegal. Throughout this period, Congress was much more concerned with abuse of alcohol than it was with drugs. This was the era that saw the rise of the temperance movement. Activists such as Carry Nation were making the headlines by leading protests against saloons. Finally, the dry movement had its way, and in 1920, the 18th Amendment to the Constitution became law, making it illegal to sell and buy alcoholic beverages in the United States.

Prohibition, which lasted 13 years, was largely a failure. Mobsters took over the beer and liquor business, smuggling it into the United States from other countries or manufacturing it in underground breweries and distilleries on American soil. The taverns may have been boarded up, but illegal clubs known as speakeasies opened for business. It is estimated that during the height of Prohibition, around 200,000 speakeasies were in operation.

Along with the speakeasies, illegal tearooms opened for business in areas such as New Orleans and New York City. The rooms served a potent tea brewed from cannabis leaves or sold cannabis cigarettes to their customers for prices as low as 25 cents per joint. The tearooms could be found in many different areas, but were especially common in poorer neighborhoods in inner cities.

It is believed that no fewer than 500 tearooms operated in the New York City neighborhood of Harlem in the 1930s.

With Prohibition nearing its repeal, Congress turned its attention to illegal drugs, establishing the Federal Bureau of Narcotics in 1930. The bureau's first director, Harry J. Anslinger, called for a federal law banning marijuana. He got his way with the adoption of the Marihuana Tax Act of 1937, which assessed

During Prohibition, if a business was caught selling alcohol, the owners could face serious charges. Authorities would also take away the alcohol. Here, a large group of men are emptying barrels of beer into a sewer.

16 The Marijuana Legalization Debate

A Sensational Film

For years, many people were under the impression that cannabis could cause insanity. This was, in part, thanks to the 1936 film *Reefer Madness*. While cannabis use has been linked to certain mental illnesses, we now know that its effects are nothing like the shocking acts shown in the movie. The film tells the outlandish story of college students who become homicidal and attempt suicide after consuming pot.

The movie was originally titled *Tell Your Children*. Produced by a church group to serve as an educational film for parents, the film tried to warn adults of the dangers of pot. However, independent film producer Dwain Esper obtained the film, reedited it, and added new scenes. Esper made the story more dramatic and renamed the film *Reefer Madness*.

The film tells a story about what happens to a group of students after they consume marijuana. One character, Bill, suffers from hallucinations. His girlfriend, Blanche, dies by suicide. Another student, Ralph, goes insane, commits a murder, and is sentenced to a psychiatric hospital.

Today, *Reefer Madness* is a cult classic. It is shown mostly on college campuses and theaters that specialize in screening art films. Rather than taking it seriously, most fans today appreciate the movie for its unintentional absurdity. It's considered campy, meaning it's so outrageous and out-of-touch that it is funny.

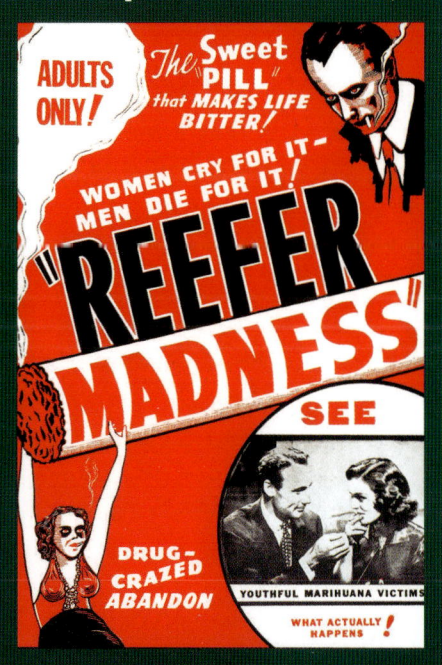

While *Reefer Madness* was initially meant to warn people about the dangers of cannabis, it eventually became a sort of joke, often enjoyed by cannabis users themselves.

Cannabis Through Time

fees on anyone who grew, sold, or prescribed marijuana. The fees themselves were small, but the process for paying them was made intentionally difficult, and the penalties for failing to file the correct paperwork were prohibitively high.

Anslinger's agents made nearly 400 arrests within the first year the law was on the books. The Bureau of Narcotics would carry on its war against marijuana for a few more years, but in 1941, America's attention was diverted to a much different war. With American troops fighting in World War II, enforcement of the laws against cannabis abuse was hardly a national priority. In fact, during World War II, hemp was grown in abundance because all raw materials were in such high demand; farmers could apply for tax stamps that allowed them to avoid paying the fees.

From Beats to Hippies

After World War II ended in 1945, men returning from the war went back to their stateside jobs, families flocked to the suburbs, and the U.S. government turned at least some of its attention back to the war against marijuana. Cannabis was added to the list of illegal drugs. The law made no distinction between marijuana and hemp. All forms of the cannabis plant were outlawed.

By the 1950s, a literary movement known as the Beat Generation was on the rise. Writers such as Jack Kerouac, Allen Ginsberg, and William S. Burroughs were heroes of the movement. The Beats wrote poetry, listened to jazz, and often smoked marijuana. New York writer Dan Wakefield recalled meeting Ginsberg in 1961 while researching a magazine story about marijuana:

> When I went to interview him, which I did several times, Allen opened a big file cabinet and pulled out reports for me to read on the medical, legal, and historical aspects of Cannabis sativa. He was eager to help anyone who would write objectively about this drug he believed should be legalized, offering facts and opinions and background information, all in a friendly, matter-of-fact manner. To my great relief, he did not use jargon or hip lingo ("Like, you know, I was uptight that he might jive me, but he was cool"), nor was he ever stoned when I

talked with him, a possibility I also feared.

Explaining the role of marijuana to the poets of his own circle, he told me that "almost everyone has experimented with it and tried writing something [while] on it. It's all part of their poetic—no, their metaphysical—education."[5]

Wakefield concluded that marijuana "was moving from the back rooms of jazz bars and coldwater pads of hipsters in Harlem and the East Village, seeping through the walls of college dormitories and into middle-class consciousness."[6] It certainly was. Within a few years, the 1960s had erupted into an era of dramatic social change. Cannabis was a big part of the counterculture movement.

College students rebelled against the authority of their parents and teachers. Campuses became hotbeds of radical thought. Students often protested against the Vietnam War. They also demonstrated in favor of civil rights, women's rights, and free speech. Thousands of "hippies" and "flower children" flocked to California, especially to San Francisco's Haight-Ashbury district and other neighborhoods where illegal drug use was often rampant. Many thought of the cannabis leaf as a symbol of rebellious youth defying their parents' authority through drug use.

Cannabis use was common at concerts and campus demonstrations. At the Woodstock Music and Art Fair in upstate New York, which was a three-day event in August 1969, the *New York Times* reported that no less than 99 percent of the crowd of 400,000 concertgoers smoked marijuana. The newspaper reported:

A billowy haze of sweet smoke rose through purple spotlights from the sloping hillside where throngs of young people—their average age about 20—sat or sprawled in the midnight darkness and listened to the rock music.

The smoke was not from the campfires.

"There was so much grass being smoked last night that you could get stoned just sitting there breathing," said a

Music festivals were—and often still are—a common place for cannabis use. This photo shows a group of people smoking the substance at the Isle of Wight Pop Festival. The event was held each year from 1968 to 1970, on an island off of southern England.

20　The Marijuana Legalization Debate

19-year-old student from Denison University in Ohio. "It got so you didn't even want another drag of anything."[7]

The concertgoers were not concerned with being punished for their actions. "They smoked quite openly, not fearing to be 'busted,' at least not within the confines of the 600-acre farm where the action is,"[8] the *Times* added. In fact, spokesmen for the New York State Police told reporters that they made few narcotics arrests that weekend. One festivalgoer who slipped through their grasp was the bass player for the band Country Joe and the Fish, who flashed his joint at a camera filming a documentary. Another headliner was folk singer Arlo Guthrie, who performed "Coming into Los Angeles" on the Woodstock stage. The song told the story of smuggling 4.4 pounds (2 kilograms) of marijuana through the U.S. customs inspection station at Los Angeles Airport. The song turned out to be a big hit for Guthrie.

Mainstream Cannabis Use

Beats and hippies were considered part of the counterculture, but it wasn't long before cannabis use moved into mainstream cultures as well. Starting in the 1960s, stores known as head shops opened in many areas. These stores sold all kinds of drug paraphernalia. Among the products found in the shops were colorful and flavored cigarette papers, commonly used by cannabis smokers to roll their own joints; glass pipes, known as bongs; and roach clips, which could hold the final remnants of a joint so that the smoke could be inhaled without burning one's fingers. By the 1970s, the head shops had moved out of urban neighborhoods and into suburban shopping centers. They were popping up all over the country. Many became popular places for teens to hang out at after school.

While police and other authority figures didn't like the shops, there was little they could do about them. The state governments had outlawed marijuana, and the federal government had acted as well. However, paraphernalia associated with the drug use had not been regulated by either the federal or state governments. As long as the shops weren't selling drugs or allowing them to be used on the premise, they weren't doing anything illegal.

By the early 1970s, however, states started passing laws prohibiting the sale of drug paraphernalia. Head shop owners were arrested, but when their cases got to court, the charges were often dismissed and the laws overruled. Courts ruled that the laws were too vague and did not specifically identify a glass pipe or roach clip as an illegal item. Indeed, most states adopted laws that merely suggested if an item could be used for the consumption of cannabis, it was illegal. Under the laws in existence at the time, the shop owners could claim that the

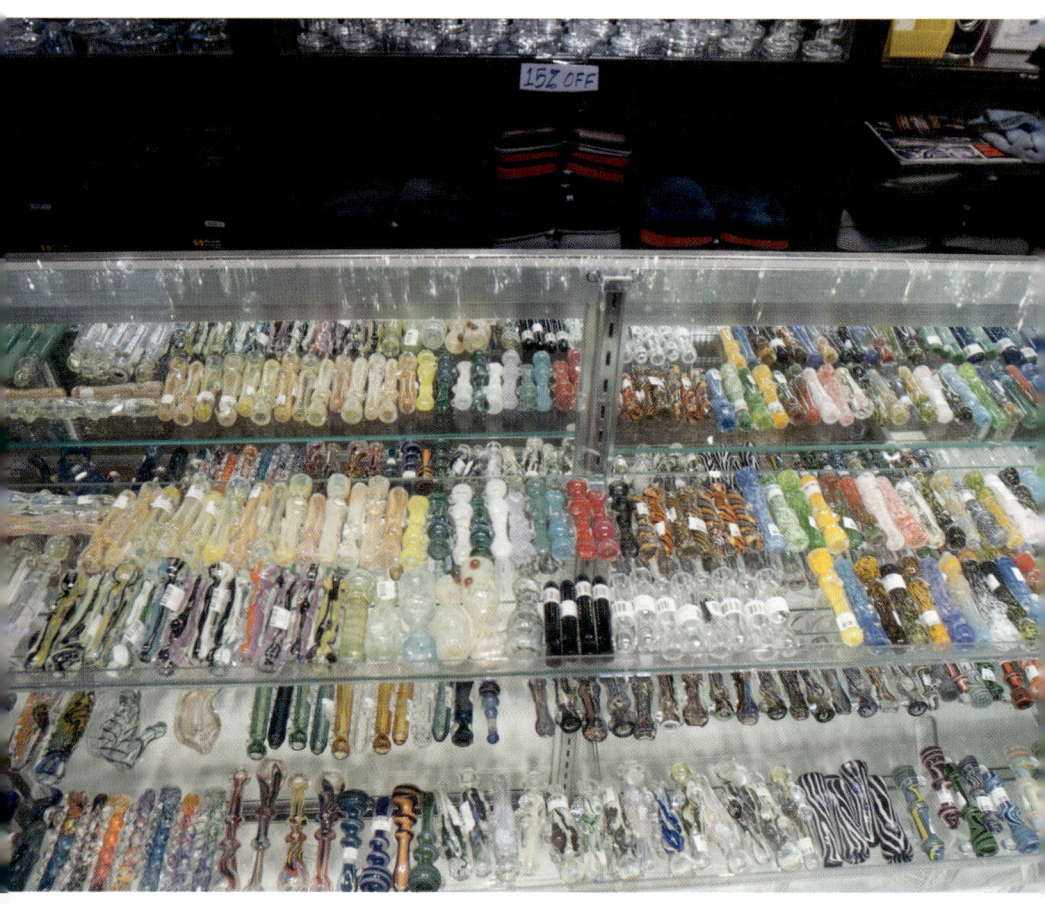

Marijuana pipes such as the ones shown here are one type of paraphernalia sold in head shops.

Operation Intercept

In 1969, the federal government conceived a plan to stop the flow of cannabis across the Mexican border. The plan, known as Operation Intercept, required U.S. customs agents to inspect every car, truck, and bus that stopped at each of the 30 border crossings located along the 1,933-mile (3,110-kilometer) Mexico-U.S. border.

The program was launched on September 21, 1969. Each day, thousands of vehicles were stopped and searched. Initially, the program produced dramatic results. In America, a genuine pot shortage developed. One Radcliffe College student told the *Wall Street Journal* that she switched to LSD because it was so hard to find cannabis. She said, "I really didn't want to try acid before, but there's no grass around, so when somebody offered me some [LSD], I figured, '[Why not?]' I didn't freak out or anything, so I've been tripping [taking LSD] ever since."[1]

Operation Intercept was halted after just 20 days. Officials were concerned that the lack of cannabis prompted drug users like the Radcliffe student to turn to more dangerous substances. Also, the searches caused tremendous traffic jams at the border crossings; motorists had to wait more than two hours for customs agents to search their vehicles. More importantly, the economy on the American side suffered. Because of the long wait at the customs stations, Mexican laborers refused to cross the border to go to their jobs in America.

1. Quoted in Edward M. Brecher, *Licit and Illicit Drugs* (Mount Vernon, NY: Consumers Union, 1972), p. 435.

---

paraphernalia had a legitimate use—every pipe, paper, bong, and roach clip on the shelves could also be used to smoke tobacco, which was legal everywhere. Judges agreed and threw out the cases against the head shop owners.

In 1979, the DEA drafted a model law that identified bongs, roach clips, and similar items as employed specifically for consumption of illegal drugs. States adopted the model laws, and in 1999, Congress passed sweeping legislation making the manufacture and sale of drug paraphernalia federal offenses punishable by up to three years in prison.

Many head shops as well as the manufacturers of paraphernalia managed to remain in business for years after the laws were adopted. As small businesses operating on the periphery of the drug trade, they were hardly regarded as priorities for police and prosecutors, who were more concerned with the growing traffic in crack cocaine and methamphetamine. Meanwhile, with the growth of the internet, paraphernalia dealers and manufacturers could remain in business while hiding behind anonymous websites. In 2003, the United States Department of Justice announced a crackdown on head shops and paraphernalia manufacturers. A program titled Operation Pipe Dreams led to the arrests of dozens of paraphernalia makers and dealers. However, only one person was sentenced to serve time in prison— Tommy Chong, an actor known for playing a bumbling pothead in several movies in the 1970s. His conviction was intended to serve as an example to other paraphernalia sellers. Aside from this arrest, the operation was largely ineffective, and although the law remains on the books, it is rare for head shops to be targeted.

Times Are Changing

Operation Pipe Dreams is just one example of how difficult it can be for authorities to keep cannabis out of the hands of Americans, even decades after the drug was first outlawed. The fact is, doing so has largely failed, and state governments are starting to come around to the idea that they will never be able to eradicate it. Additionally, state officials have started rethinking whether the drug even should be illegal. As a result, some states have chosen to legalize the drug so they can better control its sale and share in the profits by taxing it.

Known medical benefits of the drug are also being considered. Studies have shown that pot can alleviate symptoms of certain medical conditions, but similar to other substances, the potential for abuse is still present. There are also some very real and dangerous health risks involved in frequent cannabis smoking. As you can see, there are many factors that must be thought about when deciding whether or not to legalize or outlaw a substance.

Your Opinion Matters!

1. Do you think the treatment of cannabis in the United States today is similar to the Prohibition era? How so?
2. What are some potential negatives related to cannabis use?
3. Do you think governments could benefit from legalizing cannabis? How so?

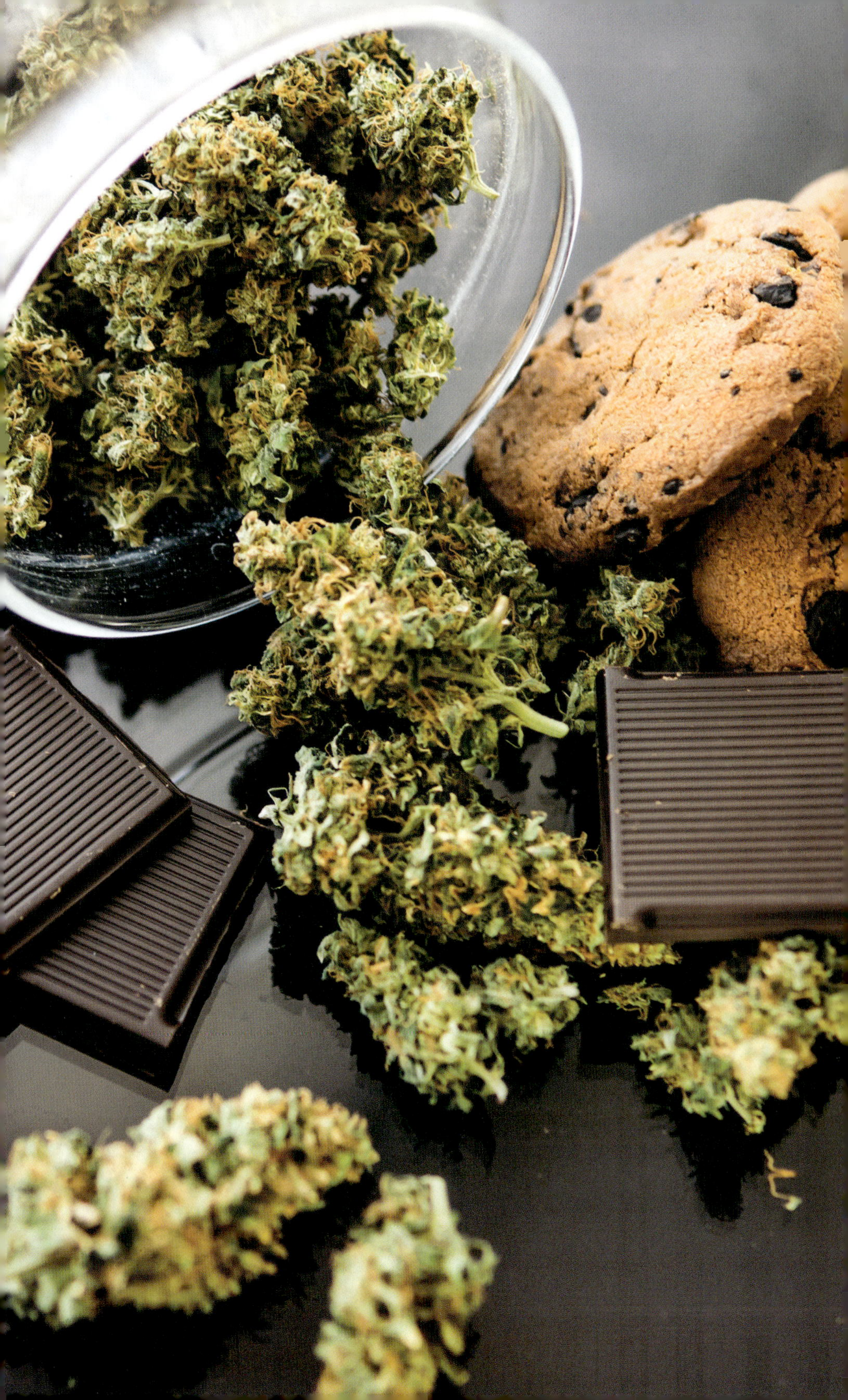

CANNABIS'S IMPACT ON THE BODY

Most people who try marijuana do it because they want to get high, or feel a type of mild euphoria caused by the drug. This high happens because THC acts on receptors in the brain that normally respond to natural chemicals that are similar to THC. THC triggers the brain's reward system, the same part of the brain that reacts when you do pleasurable activities, such as eating a food you enjoy. The brain's reward system releases a chemical called dopamine when it's expecting a reward. For example, if you know you are going to get to eat your favorite food soon, your brain may increase your dopamine levels. THC causes a similar effect, but at a much higher rate. It causes the brain to release more dopamine than natural stimuli, such as your favorite food, would release. This rush of dopamine causes the high that most recreational cannabis users are looking for. When the drug is smoked, users feel this effect very quickly. When ingested in food, the effect generally takes a bit longer to hit the user—around 30 minutes to an hour. This is because when eaten, the drug needs to first be processed through the digestive system.

While a general high is commonly reported among most cannabis users, the exact details of what each user feels can

Some people add cannabis to foods such as brownies or cookies and eat these foods to get high. These foods are commonly known as "edibles."

differ. For example, some people feel as if the level of some of their senses change; some report that they feel as if colors look brighter. Others may feel a change in their ability to think or solve problems. Many feel a change in their mood, but which direction the change goes in can differ from person to person. Some feel relaxed and at ease while others feel anxious or paranoid. These are just some of the short-term effects cannabis use has on the body. The drug also has many long-term effects, ranging from mental to physical.

THC to the Brain

When cannabis smoke is inhaled, the fumes carry the chemical THC into the lungs. The THC comes to rest on the millions of alveoli that line the lungs. These are tiny sacs that absorb oxygen and pass it into the bloodstream. Whatever is mixed in with oxygen is passed into the bloodstream as well. After being inhaled, it takes only seconds for the THC to reach the blood.

Generally, when cannabis is eaten, butter or oil is infused with pot and baked into food such as brownies or cupcakes. When the food is digested, THC enters the blood through the lining of the stomach. It takes longer for THC to be absorbed through the stomach, but once it enters the blood, the effect is stronger and lasts longer than when smoking.

The blood courses through the human body and eventually finds its way into the brain. That is where the THC meets neurotransmitters, the chemicals that deliver messages from brain cell to brain cell, affecting human behavior.

Brain cells are known as neurons; each person has billions. Each neuron emits electrical impulses containing messages that control the body's functions. To leave the neurons, impulses travel along large stems known as axons and smaller stems known as dendrites. When an impulse reaches the end of an axon, it will jump over a tiny space known as a synapse on its journey to the dendrite of the next neuron. When the electrical signal makes

Synapse

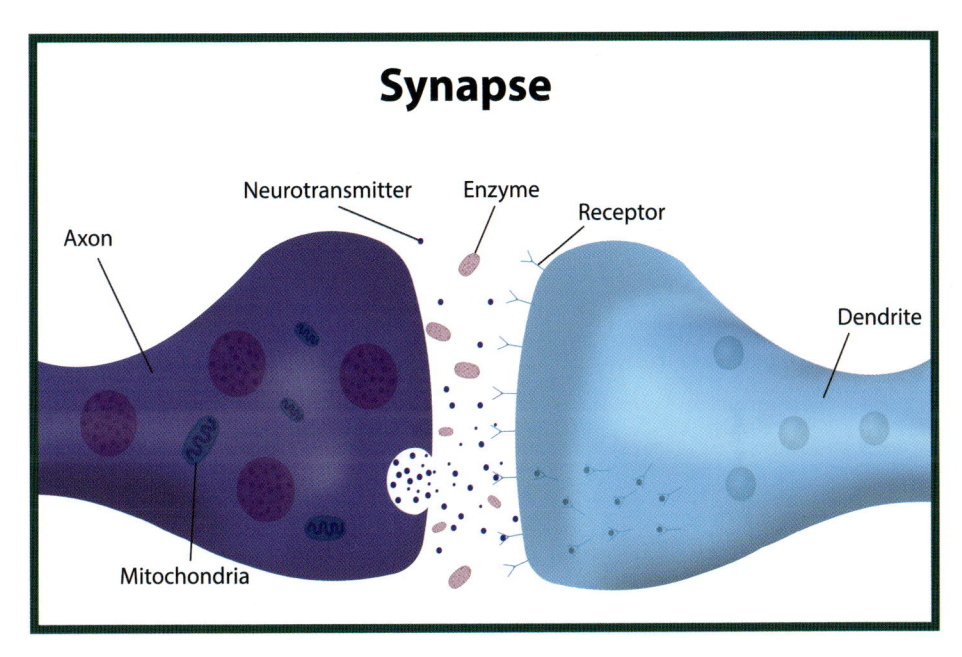

Axon · Neurotransmitter · Enzyme · Receptor · Dendrite · Mitochondria

This image shows what happens when an impulse travels across a synapse between neurons.

the jump, the brain cell releases a neurotransmitter chemical to carry the message. Accepting the message on the end of the dendrite is a group of molecules known as receptors. These receptors can only accept specific neurotransmitters. This is how the neurons of the brain work together to tell a foot to take a step, a hand to hold a pencil, or the lips to form words so that a person may speak. Not all neurotransmitters carry messages. Some neurotransmitters block unwanted messages from jumping from cell to cell.

    A drug will influence the transmission of information from neuron to neuron. The drug may produce a flood of neurotransmitters so that too many messages are delivered to the neurons; it may neutralize the neurotransmitters that work to block unwanted information, causing a flood of unwanted messages to reach the neurons; or the drug may act as its own neurotransmitter, sending its own messages to the brain cells.

When THC enters the brain, it bonds with the neurotransmitter anandamide. The combination of the two chemicals has been found to affect behavior in a number of ways. For example, as the combination of anandamide and THC jumps from neuron to neuron, it causes loss of short-term memory.

THC in low doses also promotes the brain's release of the neurotransmitter serotonin, partially responsible for giving pot smokers the dreamy, lightheaded, mellow high for which cannabis is known. As the effects wear off and serotonin leaves the system, people may feel unhappy or tired. Smoking too much can also cause the reverse effect, inhibiting serotonin to cause depression and increased risk of psychosis in people who are already genetically predisposed to it.

Dopamine is also a neurotransmitter. As discussed earlier, it creates feelings of well-being. Dopamine is a big part of why people feel happy while they are high and why they want to try it again. However, research has shown that cannabis abuse can cause people to react less strongly to dopamine when they are not high, in some cases permanently impairing the ability to react to pleasurable experiences and leading to a nearly constant general feeling of irritability.

Is It Addictive?

For years, scientists questioned whether cannabis was addictive. The answer is still controversial and often debated. Today, most experts agree addiction is more common with alcohol and other drugs, such as cocaine, than it is with cannabis. However, that doesn't mean a person can't become addicted to cannabis. Studies regarding the rate of addiction among cannabis users are sometimes disputed, but according to the Centers for Disease Control and Prevention (CDC), about 1 in 10 cannabis users become addicted. Studies also show that risk increases for people who start using the drug before age 18, with their chances of becoming addicted rising to 1 in 6, according to the CDC.

When cannabis use causes a person to have social, emotional, or physical problems, it's known as cannabis use disorder, or CUD. According to the CDC, a person can become dependent on cannabis when "the brain adapts to large amounts of the drug by reducing production of and sensitivity to its own endocannabinoid neurotransmitters."[1] While CUD is not the same as being addicted to cannabis, in serious cases, it can turn into addiction. CUD becomes addiction when a person is not able to stop using the drug even though it is causing them problems and interfering with their life.

Kevin Hill is an associate professor of psychiatry at Harvard Medical School. He has conducted research on cannabis and has written a book on the subject. In an interview with the *Harvard Gazette*, Hill pointed out that there are still many misconceptions and misunderstandings about pot, especially when it comes to addiction. Discussing cannabis addiction, he said:

> It's less addictive than alcohol, less addictive than opioids, but just because it's less addictive doesn't mean that it's not addictive. There's a subset of people — whom I treat frequently — who are using cannabis to the detriment of work, school, and relationships. It's hard for the majority of people ... to recognize the reality that there are many people who are using and losing in key areas of their lives. I've had patients who have lost multimillion-dollar careers. It's hard for people to understand that that can happen.[2]

Hill also acknowledges that while there are certainly harmful side effects related to marijuana use in general, the data can sometimes be misconstrued. When people abuse alcohol, they don't have to do it every day in order for it to be harmful, but cannabis is different. "The people who run into trouble are using it pretty much every day, multiple times a day for the most part. That's how this less-harmful, less-addictive substance turns into something that's very harmful for them,"[3] Hill said.

Hill explained that data is often collected based on heavy users, but it's not always made clear that that's the case. He points out that the dose and frequency of use is important when discussing the drug's side effects:

Young people using regularly can have cognitive problems, up to an eight-point loss of IQ over time. It can worsen depression. It can worsen anxiety. But all of those consequences depend upon the dose. The data that shows those impacts look at young people who are using pretty much every day. They're heavy users who usually meet criteria for cannabis-use disorder. So when people who are opposed to cannabis talk about those harms, they don't mention that they're talking about heavy users.[4]

However, it's still important to recognize that these side effects are serious. While becoming addicted to cannabis is far less common than becoming addicted to alcohol or other drugs, it can still happen to anyone and the potential for harm should always be considered.

Don't Smoke and Drive

In addition to causing memory loss, the combination of THC and anandamide has another significant impact on the body: loss of coordination. That is why cannabis smokers sometimes stumble around and bump into things. THC's effect on coordination can create a dangerous situation if somebody who is stoned gets behind the wheel of a car. However, this is yet another area where many people have misconceptions about how weed affects the body.

According to a 2019 study conducted by PSB Research and BuzzFeed News, nearly half of cannabis users in the United States think it is safe to drive while high on the drug. Experts, however, agree this is not the case. It's safest to drive while not impaired by any substance, including cannabis. People who are high on the drug should never get behind the wheel of a car. However, the

Drug Testing

There are many reasons why a person may be required to take a drug test. Members of high school and college sports teams are often expected to do so. Many employers require job applicants to pass drug tests before they can be hired. Also, people with certain jobs, such as those that involve operating cars or machinery, are often expected to take regular drug tests. Some employers surprise employees with random drug tests.

Cannabis can be detected in the body through urine, blood, hair, or saliva. A urine test is the most commonly administered method. Infrequent users will generally fail if they are tested within three days of their last use; the more frequent the use, the longer it takes the body to completely purge the drug. With especially heavy users, the substance may be detectable in urine for up to 30 days after use. A test of hair follicles can detect its presence up to 90 days after the last use, but this test is less commonly used because it takes longer for the drug to appear in the hair than in the urine. It is generally used to test long-term use, while a urine test is used to determine occasional or recent use.

---

level of danger driving under the influence of cannabis presents is debated.

For one thing, studies about accidents as a result of cannabis-impaired driving have produced mixed results. Several have found that there is a significantly increased risk of being involved in a crash after using cannabis. However, a study conducted by the National Highway Traffic Safety Administration found that after controlling for drivers' age, gender, race, and presence of alcohol, there was no significant increased crash risk that could be attributed to cannabis.

Additionally, unlike with drunk driving, there's no standard way to test how impaired a driver under the influence of cannabis is. Experts are not in agreement about exactly how much THC constitutes an impaired driver, and THC can stay in a person's bloodstream long after the high has gone away. Experts do agree, however, that cannabis significantly impairs a person's judgment, reaction time, and motor coordination—all things that impair a person's ability to drive safely. It is clear that driving while high can be very dangerous.

Long-Lasting Risks

Cannabis users may start coming down from their highs after two hours or so, but the drug stays in their body much longer. That is why drug tests can reveal marijuana use several days or more after the drug is consumed.

However, cannabis's impact on the human body does not stop after several days. The side effects of the drug can last much longer. Cannabis smoke contains tar, the sticky substance in cigarette smoke that sticks to the inside of the lungs, as well as other carcinogens. Heavy smokers of cannabis risk ailments commonly found among tobacco smokers—bronchitis, emphysema, and bronchial asthma. However, no proof has yet been found linking cannabis to lung cancer.

There is considerable debate over whether cannabis smokers are more or less likely to develop these conditions than tobacco smokers. Those who say it is more likely cite the fact that pot smokers tend to inhale more deeply and hold the smoke in their lungs longer than tobacco smokers do. Those who say it is less likely point out that cannabis users often smoke far less often than tobacco users. Consuming cannabis in edible or pill form significantly reduces the risk of developing one of these respiratory conditions, when compared to smoking the substance.

Women who smoke tobacco are urged to give up cigarettes if they are pregnant because the chemicals in tobacco smoke can affect the fetus. Pregnant women who smoke cannabis face similar risks. The chemicals in cannabis smoke can enhance the possibility of premature delivery. Studies show that women who smoke pot increase the risk of pregnancy complications,

normal airway   asthmatic airway

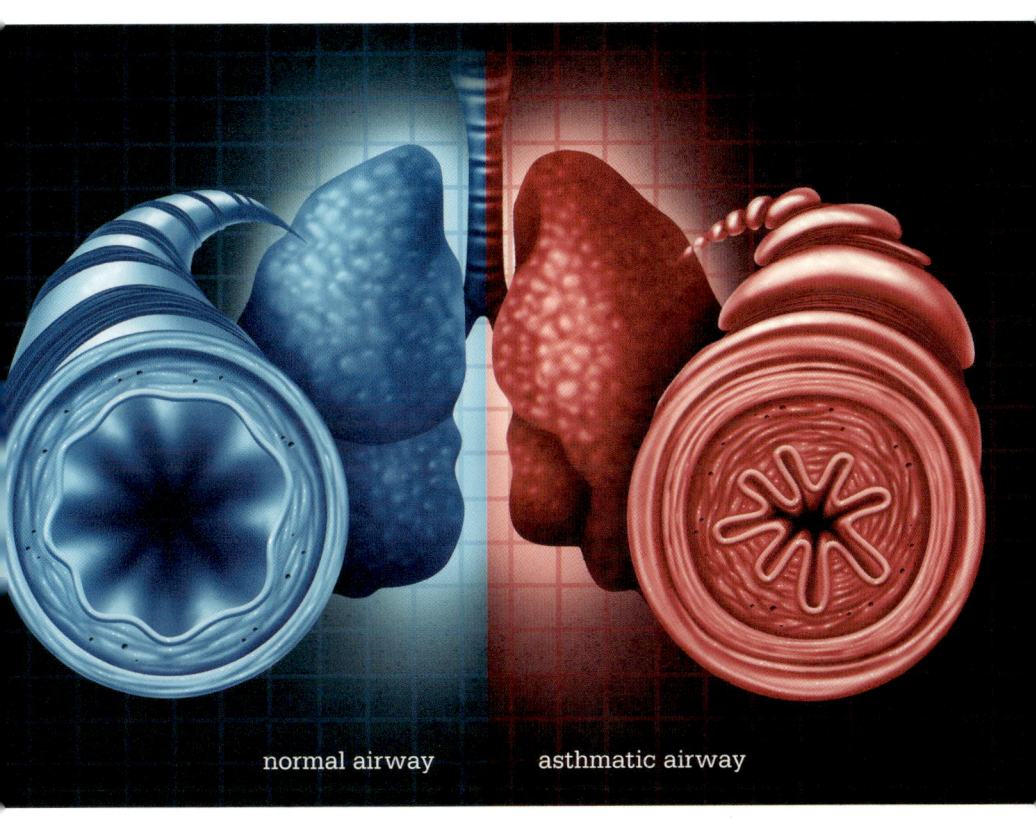

> Asthma is a condition that causes a person's airways to become inflamed and tight. This makes it difficult to breathe. If a person already has asthma, smoking can make it worse and trigger asthma attacks.

including low birth weight or even stillbirth, meaning the baby dies in the womb. Also, cannabis smoke can affect the development of the brain in fetuses, or the developing baby still in the mother's womb.

Is Cannabis a "Gateway Drug"?

For years, sociologists, physicians, and psychologists have debated whether cannabis is a gateway drug, meaning it could eventually lead to the use of much harder drugs, such as methamphetamine, cocaine, and heroin. There is still not enough research to say conclusively whether this is true, but there are several theories on

This image shows a bag of rock cocaine. It is generally agreed upon that cocaine is much more dangerous than cannabis, but some people believe cannabis could cause people to want to try more dangerous drugs such as cocaine.

both sides. One theory is that cannabis is a gateway drug because dealers who illegally supply the pot to their customers are often in the business of selling other drugs. Therefore, the dealers encourage their pot customers to experiment with harder drugs, as well. However, with the legalization of cannabis becoming more and more prevalent and legal cannabis dispensaries opening in some areas, this theory may become less relevant.

Additionally, as discussed earlier, frequent cannabis abuse decreases sensitivity to dopamine, especially when that use starts in adolescence. This may cause young adults with cannabis dependence syndrome to turn to harder drugs, looking for the good feeling they are no longer able to achieve. However, it is believed that infrequent use does not have the same effect, which means weed is not a gateway drug for adults who use it for medical purposes or occasional recreation. As with alcohol, moderation is key, and adolescents should abstain altogether to avoid weed's damaging effects, which are increased when the brain is still developing.

There is evidence to suggest that there is a correlation of cannabis users going on to use other drugs, but correlation does not imply causation. This means that just because two things occur, it does not necessarily mean that one caused the other. For example, a person who uses both cannabis and cocaine may do so because their friends use both, not because using pot made them want to try cocaine. Additionally, pot tends to be one of the easiest illegal drugs to get in the United States. It's also thought to be among the least harmful. So it makes sense that a person who is going to try illegal drugs will try pot before trying any others. Most hard drug users may have used pot before trying hard drugs, but this does not mean most pot users will go on to do hard drugs. In fact, NIDA reports that, "the majority of people who use marijuana do not go on to use other, 'harder' substances."[5] Those who do may have a genetic predisposition to addictive behaviors or may often find themselves in social situations where hard drugs are used.

Synthetic Marijuana

Synthetic marijuana or synthetic cannabinoids are drugs that combine dried, shredded herbs with synthetic, or man-made, chemicals that mimic the compounds in marijuana, such as THC and CBD. The chemicals can be sprayed onto the plants, and users can then smoke them the same way they smoke weed. These drugs may go by brand names such as Spice or K2. It is illegal to produce or possess some of the chemicals used in synthetic cannabinoids, but since they are made in a lab, the creators try to get around the laws by changing their formulas to include legal ingredients. This is why the products have sometimes been labeled as legal alternatives to marijuana and could once be purchased in some head shops or gas stations.

Regardless of whether the chemicals in a given batch are legal or illegal, synthetic cannabinoids are extremely dangerous, even though they sometimes claim to be safe alternatives to weed. They produce effects that are similar to cannabis, but stronger. They include hallucinations, confusion, extreme paranoia and anxiety, rapid heart rate, and seizures. Synthetic cannabinoids can be addictive and produce withdrawal symptoms similar to those experienced by people going through cannabis withdrawal. These products are unregulated by the government, so as with drugs such as methamphetamines and LSD, users may never be completely sure what chemicals they are inhaling. Unlike cannabis, there is no evidence of medicinal benefits from these drugs.

Changing Times

Now that cannabis is legal for recreational use in some states, and for medical use in many more, people's views on cannabis use are changing. In the past, many people considered those who regularly smoked pot incapable of contributing to society and often labeled them as lazy. Today, many respectable people are open about their recreational drug use. Medical cannabis advocates are vocal about how the drug has helped their ailments or

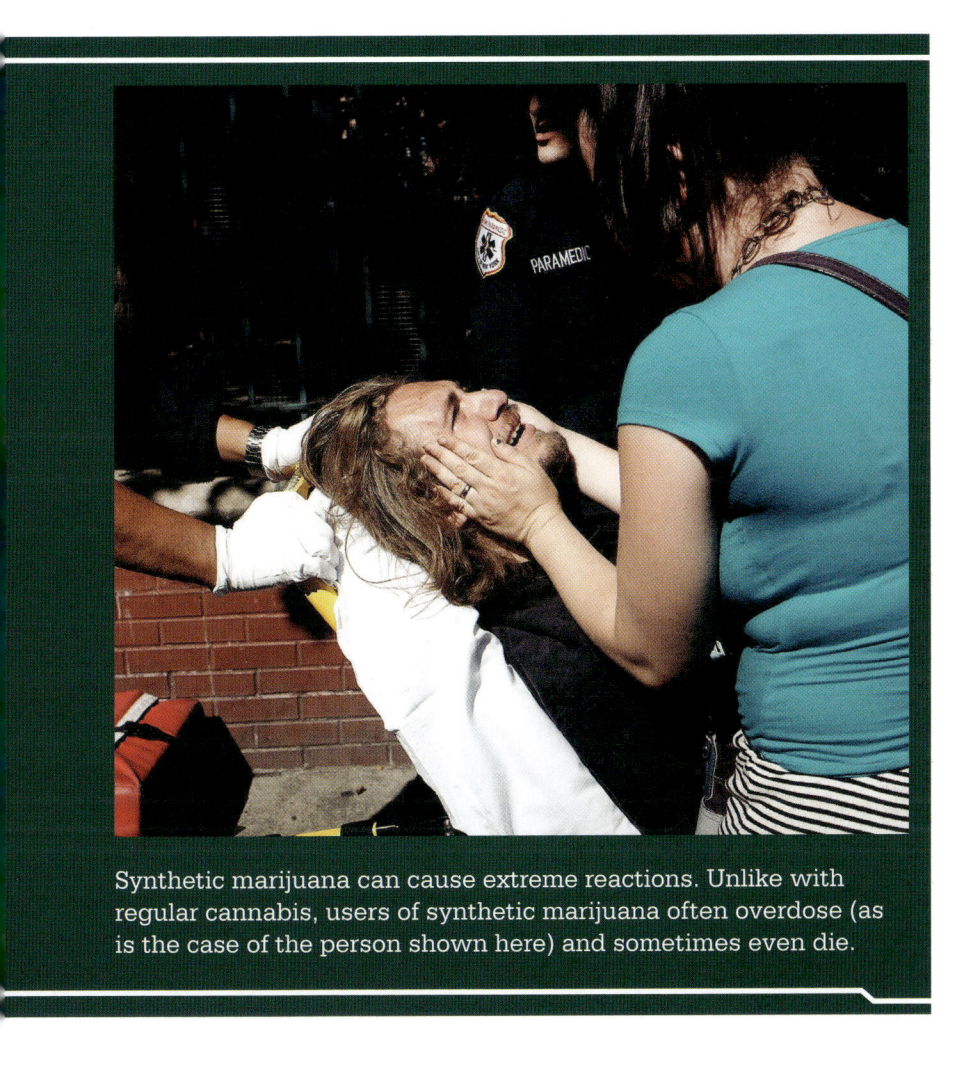

Synthetic marijuana can cause extreme reactions. Unlike with regular cannabis, users of synthetic marijuana often overdose (as is the case of the person shown here) and sometimes even die.

conditions. While there are still plenty of regulations on cannabis, in many states, legally licensed dispensaries also sell the drug to people over the age of 21, making it more accessible to the public than ever. However, even in states where it is legal, it is important for people to consider the physical and mental effects it could have before deciding to use it. And as mentioned earlier, it is much riskier for children and teenagers to use the drug than it is for adults, as their bodies are still growing and their brains

Denver, Colorado, is especially known for its legal weed dispensaries, like the one shown here.

40 The Marijuana Legalization Debate

are developing. Those under the legal age should abstain from using the drug, even in states where it is legal for adults.

Your Opinion Matters!

1. Why do you think some cannabis users think it's okay to drive under the influence of the drug?
2. Do you think cannabis is a "gateway drug"?
3. Why do you think people tend to be more accepting of cannabis now than they were in the past?

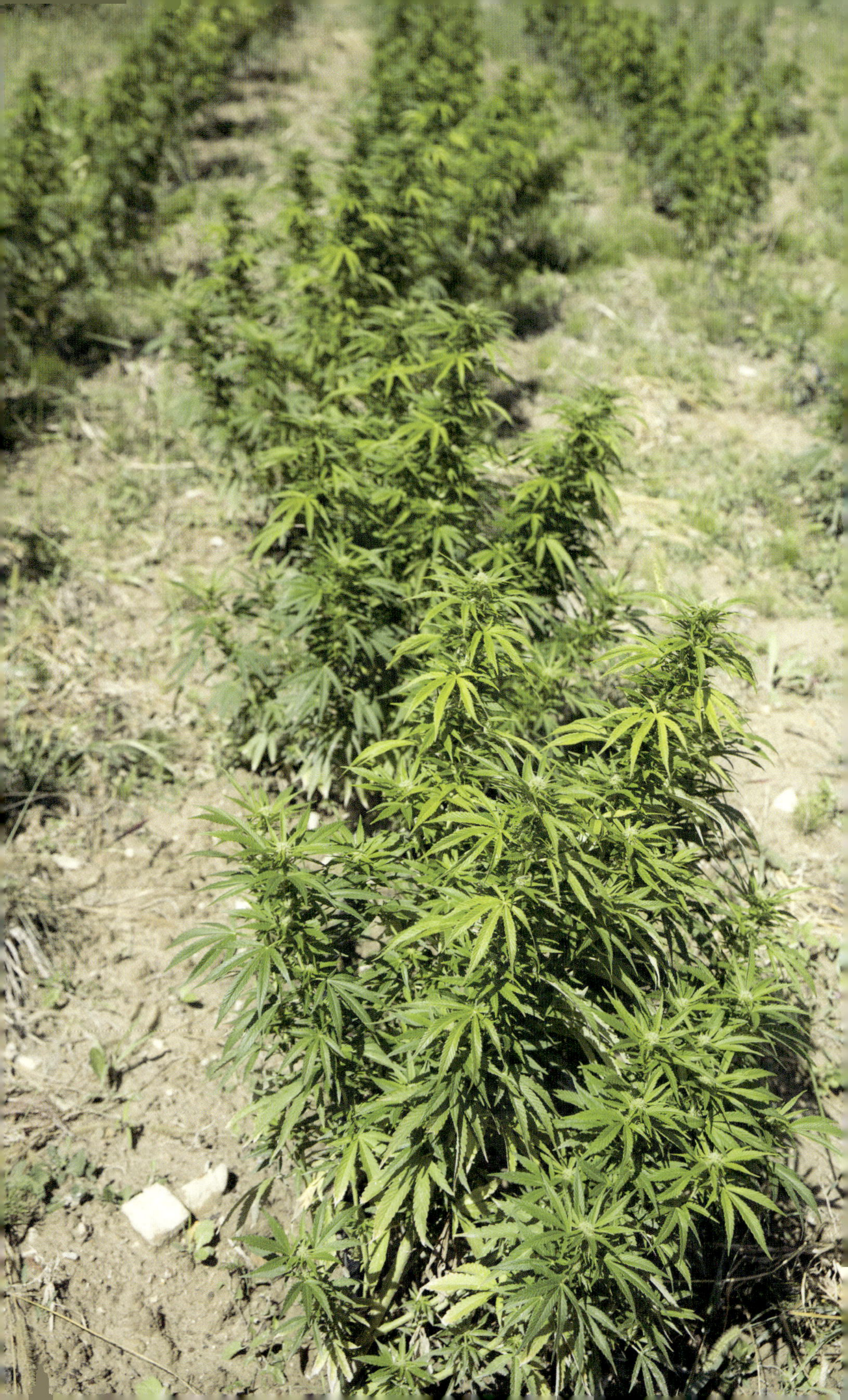

CANNABIS TODAY

Cannabis is grown illegally in every state in the United States. Even where marijuana is legal, there are many restrictions, and people still continue to grow and sell the drug unlawfully. Each state has different rules and regulations. In some states, even where recreational cannabis is legal, no one except licensed growers is allowed to grow and cultivate these plants. In other states, people may be allowed to grow the plant for their own use, but they cannot sell it to others. Some states have rules about the number of plants a person can grow at a time and where they can grow them. For example, in some states, growers cannot grow the plant in an open space such as a backyard. Cannabis can, however, be found growing illegally all over the country—from basements, where bright artificial lights mimic the sunlight needed for plant growth, to large fields hidden deep in the country, where the growers believe authorities are unlikely to find it.

Across Borders

Although police often find cannabis growing in the United States, the drug is also imported into the country by being smuggled across the borders in a variety of ways. Cannabis is

◀ Cannabis plants are grown both legally and illegally all over the world. In some places, the plants even grow naturally in the wild.

grown all over the world. In the United States, imported cannabis sometimes comes from Mexico and other Latin American countries, as well as Caribbean nations such as Jamaica. Thailand is also regarded as a major cannabis-producing country. These are places where the tropical climate and rich soil combine to make ideal conditions for the cultivation of the plant.

When it comes to growing the drug, a tropical climate is not necessary, but it helps. Cannabis is a hardy and vigorous plant, capable of growing wherever there is soil, sun, and rain. Indeed, cannabis is grown in abundance in Canada, a country with a short growing season due to its cold climate. Now that cannabis is legal in Canada, Americans who live near the border sometimes attempt to purchase the drug there and illegally bring it back home. Smugglers often bring large amounts into the country with the intent to sell and make a profit. The most common method smugglers use to bring cannabis into the United States is to drive it across the Mexican and Canadian borders. Each day, tens of thousands of cars and trucks drive through the many United States customs stations along the two borders. Border patrol agents inspect many vehicles, but there are simply not enough inspectors or enough time to look through each car and truck that stops at the border.

In recent years, the number of border patrol agents looking through cars and trucks at the borders has grown, causing smugglers to resort to other means to bring drugs into the country. Boats and planes are used, certainly, but the National Drug Intelligence Center reports that cars and trucks are still the major method of bringing cannabis into the United States. According to the agency, if the smugglers decide not to chance a crossing at a border patrol station, they can easily employ an off-road vehicle to drive across the thousands of miles of open wilderness that are available along the Canadian and Mexican borders. A report by the agency said:

> The transportation of marijuana from foreign source areas to the United States, as well as the transportation of

foreign and domestic marijuana within the United States, occurs overwhelmingly by land. Transportation also occurs by sea and air; however, smugglers continue to exploit the breadth of the U.S. land borders with Mexico and Canada, transporting huge amounts of marijuana via official border checkpoints as well as countless unofficial crossing points.[1]

In recent years, drug smugglers have turned to other means to sneak the drug across the borders. Since 1990, drug agents have uncovered more than 168 tunnels dug beneath the Mexican and Canadian borders. In early 2016, authorities uncovered a tunnel 0.5 miles (0.8 km) long, stretching from Tijuana, Mexico, to the town of Otay Mesa, California, just across the border. Inside the tunnel, police found several thousand pounds of marijuana and cocaine awaiting shipment. Six people were arrested on smuggling charges. At the time, authorities said it was the longest, narrowest tunnel they had found in California.

Cannabis-Selling Cartels

While it's still illegal federally, one welcome effect of cannabis legalization in many parts of the United States has been the decline in the amount of cannabis being imported from other countries. It is now safer and easier for people to get their weed, both legally and illegally, from growers in the United States. This removes some of the financial support for violent drug cartels, although these groups still control the cocaine and heroin trades, as well as about one-third of the cannabis trade.

In some cases, the profits from cannabis sales are used to support political causes. In the South American country of Colombia, such profits have reportedly been used to fund groups such as the Revolutionary Armed Forces of Colombia, the National Liberation Army, and the United Self-Defense Forces of Colombia. Each group requires large sums of money to buy arms for their insurgent rebels, who seek to topple the Colombian government.

Elsewhere, cannabis exports are managed by drug lords who harbor no revolutionary causes and are instead interested in nothing more than money. Before he died in a shoot-out with Mexican police in 1987, the drug lord Pablo Acosta headed an organization responsible for smuggling tons of cannabis into the United States—often hidden beneath shipments of cantaloupes trucked across the border. Another drug lord, Rafael Caro Quintero, presided over a cannabis plantation, known as Rancho Búfalo, in the Mexican state of Chihuahua. The plantation covered 1,344 acres (540 hectares). It was shut down in 1985 after the murder of DEA agent Enrique Camarena, who discovered the operation. Caro Quintero was sentenced to 40 years in prison on murder charges.

Perhaps the most well-known drug lord from recent years is Joaquín Guzmán, also known as El Chapo. In the late 1980s, Guzmán became a leader in the Sinaloa drug cartel, based in Mexico. Under his direction, the cartel produced and smuggled drugs including cannabis, cocaine, and heroin across the U.S.-Mexico border. After being arrested in 1993, Guzmán continued running the cartel from prison. In 2001, he escaped with help from corrupt prison workers. It was believed that around this time, Guzmán was responsible for most of the cannabis and cocaine that came to the United States from Colombia and Mexico. In February 2014, Guzmán was arrested again. However, in July 2015, he escaped from prison once more. He wasn't recaptured until January 2016. He was turned over to U.S. authorities in 2017. His trial began in November 2018, and he was found guilty in February 2019. Later that year, Guzmán was sentenced to life in prison. In February 2021, Guzmán's wife, Emma Coronel Aispuro, was arrested and charged with participating in a conspiracy to distribute cannabis and other drugs for unlawful importation into the United States.

Joaquín "El Chapo" Guzmán is shown here in police custody in Mexico in 2014.

Authorities eventually caught up with Acosta, Caro Quintero, and Guzmán. As cannabis becomes less profitable for cartels, many are concentrating more on cocaine and heroin. This means that cannabis users are less likely to be funding violent crime by buying pot, although it is still a possibility when that pot is obtained illegally. State regulations ensure that the weed being sold by registered dispensaries is ethically grown and distributed.

Pot in the Public Eye

Today, cannabis use is more accepted than at any point in recent history. Many people are quite open about using the substance. In fact, the list of celebrities who admit to cannabis use is rather long. Occasionally, some have been arrested for possession of the drug. Among them is actor Matthew McConaughey, who was arrested after police responded to his neighbors' noise complaints and found paraphernalia in his house.

Olympic swimmer Michael Phelps was not arrested when a photograph of him smoking weed surfaced in 2009, but he suffered repercussions to his career: USA Swimming suspended him for three months, and one of his sponsors said it would not renew his contract. The rapper Dr. Dre has long professed a devotion to cannabis. One of his biggest records, *The Chronic*, included several rap songs that praised the use of pot. "Chronic" is a street term for a particularly potent strain of marijuana.

Another singer who has glorified cannabis is country singer Willie Nelson. The cover of his album *Countryman* featured green cannabis leaves—a design that prompted Wal-Mart to ban sales of the record in its stores. Nelson has never been secretive about his love for cannabis. In the late 1970s, he claimed to have smoked cannabis in the White House, where he was staying as a guest of President Jimmy Carter's family. In 1995, he was arrested in Texas when police found pot in his

In 2020, Matthew McConaughey, shown here, came out with a memoir that detailed his 1999 arrest, among other parts of his life.

Cannabis Today

car. A judge later ruled that the search violated Nelson's rights, and the charges were dropped.

Then, there is the story of Paul McCartney, the famous singer who was arrested in 1980 at a Japanese airport when customs inspectors found 0.5 pounds (226 grams) of pot hidden in his suitcase. McCartney spent nine days in jail before he was released and kicked out of the country. At the time, McCartney was on a world tour with his band Wings, which he formed after leaving the Beatles. Angrily, McCartney declared he would never again play a concert in Japan. Years later, he recalled, "I was out in New York and I had all this really good grass. We were about to fly to Japan and I knew I wouldn't be able to get anything to smoke over there. This stuff was too good to flush down the toilet, so I thought I'd take it with me."[2] McCartney has said he has since given up cannabis.

Today, many celebrities, from comedians such as Seth Rogen and Pete Davidson to singers such as Lady Gaga and Miley Cyrus, talk openly about their use of cannabis. Even politicians, including multiple presidents, have admitted to using the drug during their lifetimes.

Who Uses Cannabis?

When celebrities such as Miley Cyrus or Seth Rogen talk about their cannabis habits, it ends up all over the internet. However, statistics show that millions of regular Americans smoke pot too. In fact, according to the NIDA, nearly 12 million young adults in the United States reported using cannabis in the year 2018. However, it's not only adults who use the drug. The Monitoring the Future (MTF) Survey has measured drug and alcohol use among adolescent students around the United States since 1975. It is conducted by the University of Michigan, with funding from the NIDA. In 2020, the survey found that 43.7 percent of 12th graders had tried cannabis at some point in their lifetime. Meanwhile, 33.3 percent of 10th graders

Comedy movies that focus on cannabis use are often called "stoner comedies." John Cho (*right*) and Kal Penn (*left*) played stoners Harold and Kumar in a popular film series between 2004 and 2011.

and 14.8 percent of eighth graders admitted to trying it at some point. However, only 1.1 percent of eighth graders reported using the drug daily, whereas 4.4 percent of 10th graders and 6.9 percent of 12th graders reported using the drug daily.

Many young cannabis users use vaporizers, better known simply as vapes or vape pens, to use the drug. Of those students who reported having tried cannabis, more than two

Cannabis Today 51

This photo shows a 64-year-old woman looking at cannabis products to buy in Denver. Cannabis users are a variety of ages.

thirds of those in the 8th or 10th grade groups said they had vaped it. Just under two thirds of the 12th grade group reported the same.

Perhaps to the surprise of some young people, older adults use cannabis too. According to a study published in the Journal of the American Medical Association in 2020, the rate of adults over age 65 who reported using cannabis in the past year increased from 2.4 percent in 2015 to 4.2 percent in 2018. Many older adults are prescribed medical cannabis for illnesses, but others choose to use the drug recreationally.

Still Debated

Not all cannabis that is either homegrown or smuggled into the country is used for recreational purposes. In fact, many people who smoke cannabis do not do it to get high from the drug, but rather to help ease the painful symptoms they suffer from due to debilitating diseases or conditions. Many effects of the drug have been endorsed by health-care professionals as acceptable treatments for pain and other ramifications of disease. For example, the dreamy, euphoric high that makes it hard for people to concentrate can also serve as an analgesic, meaning it is an effective painkiller. That can be an enormous benefit to cancer patients and others who suffer from long-term pain. Also, cannabis's propensity for making people hungry has surfaced as a treatment for the sufferers of acquired immunodeficiency syndrome, or AIDS, as well as for those undergoing chemotherapy, which is the aggressive use of chemicals to kill cancer cells. In many cases, AIDS and chemotherapy patients lose their appetites and suffer from malnutrition. By smoking cannabis, though, many of them regain the desire to eat.

As discussed earlier, medical uses for cannabis go back thousands of years. However, while most states in the United States have now legalized cannabis for medical purposes, for a long time it was illegal for people in the country to use the drug as a

Religious Uses

Several religions use cannabis to help their members perform acts of worship. For example, during holidays, some Hindus consume bhang, which is a paste made from cannabis. This paste is often mixed with milk and spices to produce a drink or with sugar and ghee (clarified butter) to make a type of candy. They believe bhang helps them worship the Hindu god Shiva.

Hindus who found work as farm laborers in Jamaica during the 1800s introduced cannabis to the island. In the 1930s, the use of cannabis was embraced by a small Jamaican religious sect known as the Rastafarians, who believe cannabis opens their minds and helps them worship Haile Selassie, who became the emperor of Ethiopia in 1930 and whom Rastafarians believe to be a god. Despite their use of the substance for religious purposes, Rastafarians living in Jamaica, the United States, and elsewhere have been prosecuted on drug offenses and were often made to serve prison sentences. However, as of 2015, Jamaica has decriminalized possession of small amounts of cannabis and legalized it for religious use. The United States has not yet legalized cannabis for this purpose.

Bhang is commonly used in the Hindu spring festival of Holi. During Holi, people also gather and throw colored powders, each color holding a special meaning.

kind of medicine. Those who needed the drug to feel better had to get it illegally. Even today, there is still debate over whether people should be allowed to ease the effects of their illnesses using cannabis. Some people do not think the drug should be used for any reason. There is, however, more acceptance today for medical cannabis than ever before in recent history.

Your Opinion Matters!

1. Why do you think cannabis is most commonly smuggled into the United States by car over the borders?
2. Can you think of any positive or negative effects of celebrities talking about their cannabis use?
3. Why do you think vaping has become a more popular way of consuming cannabis for young people?

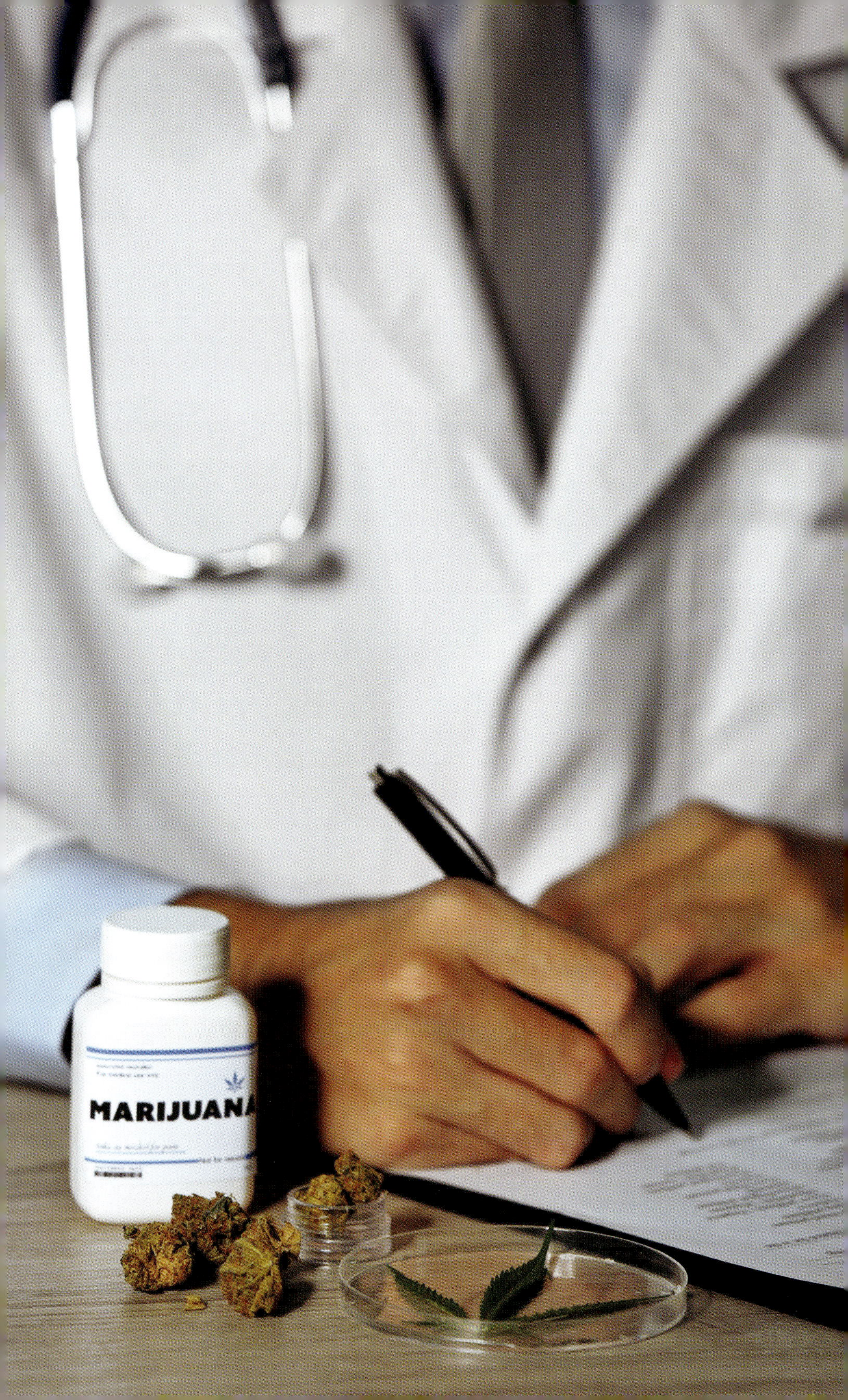
MARIJUANA

CHAPTER FOUR
MEDICAL USES

People all around the world have used cannabis to treat a variety of conditions, including nausea, insomnia, and migraines, for thousands of years. Even in the United States, where it is currently federally illegal for all uses, doctors recommended it to patients to help ease certain ailments right up until the Marihuana Tax Act of 1937 was passed. Today, due to widespread state legalization, many doctors are able to do so again.

While some people want legalized cannabis so they can get high without the threat of legal ramifications, that's not the case for many others. For these people, legalizing cannabis isn't about getting high, it's about allowing people to ease painful symptoms of many different ailments. When the AIDS epidemic began in the 1980s, it was discovered that cannabis helped patients regain the appetite that AIDS took from them, helping them eat more so they would not suffer from malnutrition. This caused many gay people, who were affected by the AIDS epidemic in large numbers, and their friends and families to campaign for cannabis legalization.

After several studies were done by the American Medical Association (AMA), enough evidence was gathered to convince several states to legalize cannabis for medical use only.

◄ Today, doctors in many states can once again legally prescribe cannabis to their patients.

A Federal Cannabis Program?

Federal prosecutors have ordered the arrests of medical cannabis growers, but at one time, the government believed cannabis did have promise as a drug that could treat pain and other symptoms of disease. In 1976, the United States Food and Drug Administration (FDA) established the experimental Compassionate Investigational New Drug program. The program provided cannabis cigarettes to a handful of patients to gauge their reactions to the drug.

The first patient admitted under the program was a glaucoma sufferer. The disease causes painful pressure on the eyes, and studies have shown that cannabis helps ease the pain. By 1992, the program was flooded with applicants who wished to participate. Rather than expand the program, the administration of President George H. W. Bush elected to close it to new applicants, although the dozen or so patients already in the program continued to receive their government-grown pot, which is cultivated in a closely guarded field at the University of Mississippi. By 2012, just four patients were still part of the program. At least one has since passed away. While some members of the program chose to remain anonymous, several were quite outspoken about the benefits they saw from the government-provided cannabis.

Even today, in states where only medical cannabis is legal, a doctor must prescribe patients with it, and many often only do so after all other options have been exhausted. Laws vary from state to state regarding whether patients are allowed to have a smokable or non-smokable supply, as well as whether or not they are allowed to grow their own plants.

As pot continues to gain mainstream popularity, more studies will be conducted, and new research will continue to emerge. What we know about cannabis right now could very well be proven wrong in a few years' time. However, the vast majority of medical cannabis users believe that the benefits they receive from using the drug far outweigh any ill effects they may experience. Many scientists and medical experts agree.

California Starts a Wave

The state of California has been a driving force behind the cannabis legalization movement. This, especially in the movement's early days, has largely been thanks to the state's gay population. San Francisco, in particular, had been hit hard during the AIDS epidemic. In 1991, gay activists organized the drive to slate Proposition P on the ballot in San Francisco. The ballot question asked voters whether California should legalize medical cannabis. The measure passed with 80 percent of the vote. Since Proposition P was limited to the city of San Francisco, it had no effect on California's state laws banning cannabis use; it merely proved to government officials that the majority of San Francisco citizens supported statewide legalization.

Still, the activists were encouraged by the response from San Francisco voters, and they urged the city's board of supervisors to adopt a resolution decriminalizing medical cannabis. The supervisors agreed, passing a resolution that stated, "San Francisco Police and the District Attorney will place as its lowest priority enforcement of marijuana laws that interfere with the medical application of this valued herb."[1]

However, many medical cannabis activists were not satisfied with their victory in San Francisco. Following the adoption of Proposition P, activists organized a statewide movement to convince the California Assembly that medical cannabis should be legalized. In 1996, they succeeded in slating a statewide ballot question asking voters to approve Proposition 215, also known as the California Compassionate Use Act, legalizing the use of cannabis by anyone who obtains the recommendation of a physician for treatment of "cancer, anorexia, AIDS, chronic fatigue, spasticity, glaucoma, arthritis, migraine headaches, or any other illness for which marijuana provides relief."[2]

Voters approved the measure, making California the first state to legalize medical cannabis. Within a few years, nine more states—Alaska, Arizona, Colorado, Hawaii, Maine, Montana, Nevada, Oregon, and Washington—had enacted similar laws. Many other states only decriminalized cannabis at first, then legalized it for medical use after several more years had passed. Legalization has only continued to grow. As of February 2021, 36 states, plus Washington, D.C., Guam, Puerto Rico, and the U.S. Virgin Islands have approved medical cannabis programs. Fifteen states have legalized the use of recreational cannabis, as have Washington, D.C., and Guam. Several states allow CBD with low THC levels, but do not allow cannabis for either medical or

States have their own regulations on medical cannabis. Many limit the amount of medical cannabis a person can have on them at one time.

recreational purposes. As of February 2021, cannabis was only illegal in eight states in the entire United States. Even still, several of these states had already decriminalized it.

Who Can Benefit?

Numerous studies have supported that there are medical benefits of using cannabis. As stated earlier, the drug's propensity for making its users hungry could be an enormous benefit to AIDS sufferers, who are often made nauseated by the disease as well as the harsh drugs used to treat the condition. Likewise, cancer patients forced to endure chemotherapy could also benefit from consuming cannabis. Chemotherapy can be an effective treatment, but when patients' bodies are bombarded by the chemicals, they often grow ill and nauseated and have difficulty keeping their food down. Research has found that cannabis can help with this and other effects of cancer.

Multiple sclerosis patients were also found to benefit from consuming cannabis. These patients suffer from spasticity, meaning their muscles grow rigid. Cannabis relaxes their muscles and gives them freedom of movement, according to the AMA.

The AMA also found that glaucoma patients could get relief from cannabis. Cannabis was found to ease the pressure suffered by glaucoma patients. However, in this case, the AMA cautioned that cannabis may not be the right medicine for many glaucoma sufferers. Since many glaucoma patients are elderly, the association said, caution should be urged in the use of cannabis because the drug can also cause the pulse to race, a potentially fatal side effect for elderly users. Some experts have also noted that there are a number of other drugs that have been shown to be more effective and last longer in treating glaucoma side effects than medical cannabis.

The most common use of medical cannabis in the United States is to treat pain. For years, medical researchers have struggled to develop effective analgesics, and scientific improvements have allowed for them to do just that. Many highly effective drugs can be prescribed today for severe pain. In most cases, however, those treatments are drawn from the class of drugs known as opioids, which can be highly addictive. In fact, the illegal and addictive drug heroin is an opioid. While cannabis does have addictive qualities, most experts agree it is far less addictive than most opioids. In the *Harvard Health Blog*, Dr. Peter Grinspoon noted:

> *While marijuana isn't strong enough for severe pain ... it is quite effective for the chronic pain that plagues millions of Americans, especially as they age. Part of its allure is that it is clearly safer than opiates (it is impossible to overdose on and far less addictive) and it can take the place of [drugs] such as Advil or Aleve.*[3]

Grinspoon also noted that cannabis is said to be a great muscle relaxer, effective in treating those with tremors due to Parkinson's disease, as well as many other conditions that result in chronic pain.

While there is much evidence to support the benefits of medical cannabis, new studies and research are being done all the time. It's entirely possible that some of the findings mentioned in this book will be disputed and possibly disproven in the future. Likewise, it's possible doctors and scientists will find new uses for the drug. People considering medical cannabis should speak about it openly with their doctors to find the best treatment for them.

Opponents and Non-Smoked Cannabis

Many advocates continue to applaud scientific research supporting cannabis as an effective medical remedy as more and more of it comes out. Yet the concept of legalizing pot for medical purposes still has its critics. Sheryl Massaro, former spokesperson for NIDA, said that legalizing marijuana for medical reasons could suggest to people that using pot for recreational purposes

Opiates, including heroin, come from the opium poppy plant and its seedpods, shown here.

is acceptable and harmless. "Seeming to legalize marijuana for anything would give young people the wrong impression," she said. "That doesn't even seem to enter the minds of a lot of people who are promoting it for medical use."[4]

Billy R. Martin, former pharmacology professor at the Medical College of Virginia, insisted that there are many legitimate drugs that can provide the same benefits as cannabis. In addition to the well-known painkillers, Martin said, pharmaceutical companies have developed drugs to counter the nausea brought on by AIDS and chemotherapy. "There are better drugs out there,"[5] he said.

In order to combat these types of concerns, as well as reduce the negative effects smoking has on the lungs, a drug called Marinol was developed in the 1980s. It incorporates THC into a pill form. Marinol was the forerunner of the modern medical cannabis movement. It is still sometimes prescribed, but other forms of non-smokable cannabis have since been developed and are more widely used.

Critics believe Marinol and other pill-like methods have their shortcomings and are far less effective than smoking cannabis. For example, since they enter the blood through the stomach lining, pills take far more time to work. Asking an AIDS or cancer patient to spend a few more minutes waiting for relief may not seem like much to ask, but the patient who is enduring chronic nausea or gut-wrenching vomiting may disagree. University of Arizona pharmacology professor Paul Consroe said another important difference between Marinol and pot is that a medical cannabis smoker needs to smoke only enough of the drug to find relief, whereas a Marinol user gets the full jolt of whatever is in the pill. He said, "With smoked marijuana, patients get immediate relief, whereas with the oral drug they get a delayed, big rush of unpleasantness. When they take a small dose [of Marinol] it doesn't work."[6]

One method that addresses these problems is to administer cannabis as a tincture—extracting the active compounds into a liquid form and applying it under the tongue. In this way, supporters claim, "tinctures enter the bloodstream immediately, allowing for fast-acting effects and better dose control."[7] Tinctures are a common way people take CBD, but cannabis tinctures with higher amounts of THC are also widely available and used.

Many people against medical cannabis oppose it because, even if it benefits patients, it still has the side effect of getting them stoned or high. Critics say this makes them unable to function in everyday life, particularly at work or school. These non-smokable methods solve that problem because they are so low in THC that they generally do not get the user high. In some states where medical cannabis is legal, it is still only legally available to have in these non-smokable and non-edible methods.

States Face the Feds

In 2002, U.S. attorney general John Ashcroft declared that he would crack down on medical cannabis growers. Ashcroft insisted that the 1970 federal Controlled Substances Act took precedence over the state laws that permitted cannabis for medical purposes, meaning that whatever the laws of the states that had legalized the substance permitted, growing, selling, and using cannabis for medical purposes was still illegal under federal law. He directed the DEA to investigate and arrest medical cannabis growers.

The DEA responded that year by raiding the home of Diane Monson, who grew cannabis in her backyard garden in Oroville, California. Monson started smoking pot to ease her own chronic back pain. In the raid on Monson's garden, the DEA seized six plants. Monson fought back, asking the courts to prohibit the Justice Department from prosecuting the growers and users of medical cannabis. Monson enlisted Angel Raich, an outspoken supporter of legalization, as an ally. The two women filed a lawsuit against the Justice Department, arguing that the federal government could not enforce the Controlled Substances Act in states that had adopted medical cannabis laws.

Angel Raich is shown here speaking to a group of students at the University of Montana on April 20, 2007. April 20, or 4/20, has become known as a sort of cannabis holiday around the United States. The students here are demonstrating for rights of cannabis users.

66　The Marijuana Legalization Debate

A federal judge rejected the women's claim and refused to bar the Justice Department from enforcing the Controlled Substances Act on medical cannabis growers, but in 2003, an appeals court sided with Monson and Raich. The appeals court said that Congress, which enacted the Controlled Substances Act, exceeded its authority by prohibiting use of a medically advantageous drug. At that point, the Justice Department appealed the case to the U.S. Supreme Court. Arguments were held before the court in November 2004; seven months later, the court issued its opinion. The court ruled that the federal government does have the power under the 1970 law to prosecute growers and users of medical cannabis, despite what state laws may allow.

In 2013, during President Barack Obama's administration, a policy was passed by the Justice Department that blocked the federal government from prosecuting federal cannabis-related crimes in states where cannabis had been legalized and such actions were not illegal according to state laws. The policy said federal prosecutions were only to go forward in possession cases that involved distribution to minors, gangs, organized crime, sales across state borders, or unauthorized cultivation of cannabis plants on federal land. However, in 2018, under Donald Trump's administration, Attorney General Jeff Sessions reversed this policy, allowing the federal government to again enforce federal laws against cannabis—even in states where it was fully legal. In more recent years, the federal government has mostly turned its attention to other matters, but unless cannabis is legalized at the federal level, the federal government could focus on this issue again at any time.

Federal Cannabis Legalization?

In writing the Supreme Court's opinion regarding Monson and Raich's case, Justice John Paul Stevens said it is clear that AIDS and cancer victims and other sufferers of debilitating diseases have valid reasons for wanting to use medical cannabis. Stevens said

Mental Health Benefits?

While cannabis has become increasingly popular and several studies have backed up its effectiveness on physical health, there is still much more to be learned about the substance when it comes to mental health benefits. More studies and research are constantly being carried out. For years, there were very few thorough studies on its alleged mental health benefits. However, people have used cannabis illegally for years to treat the symptoms of conditions such as anxiety, depression, obsessive-compulsive disorder (OCD), attention deficit/hyperactivity disorder (ADHD), Alzheimer's disease, insomnia, and more. Some users claim it helps with the effects of these conditions tremendously. However, some people say they've experienced worsening of certain symptoms when consuming cannabis.

Many people swear by CBD as an effective relief from certain mental conditions, such as depression. Since it doesn't contain enough THC to get users high, many say they've experienced calmness and eased symptoms with no increase of other symptoms, such as anxiety or paranoia, that THC can sometimes bring about. However, experts are still in the process of studying CBD and its effectiveness as a medical remedy. While many patients report positive effects of using CBD, more studies need to be done to scientifically confirm its benefits.

---

he was moved by the afflictions that plagued Raich (cancer) and Monson. Nevertheless, Stevens said, it is evident that the amount of cannabis grown in the United States and imported from other countries is far in excess of what medical cannabis users require. Clearly, Stevens said, if the court permitted the production of medical cannabis, it would not take long for the pot to wind up in the wrong hands. "The likelihood that all such production ... will precisely match the patients' needs ... seems remote, whereas the danger that excesses will satisfy some of the admittedly enormous demand for recreational use seems obvious,"[8] he said.

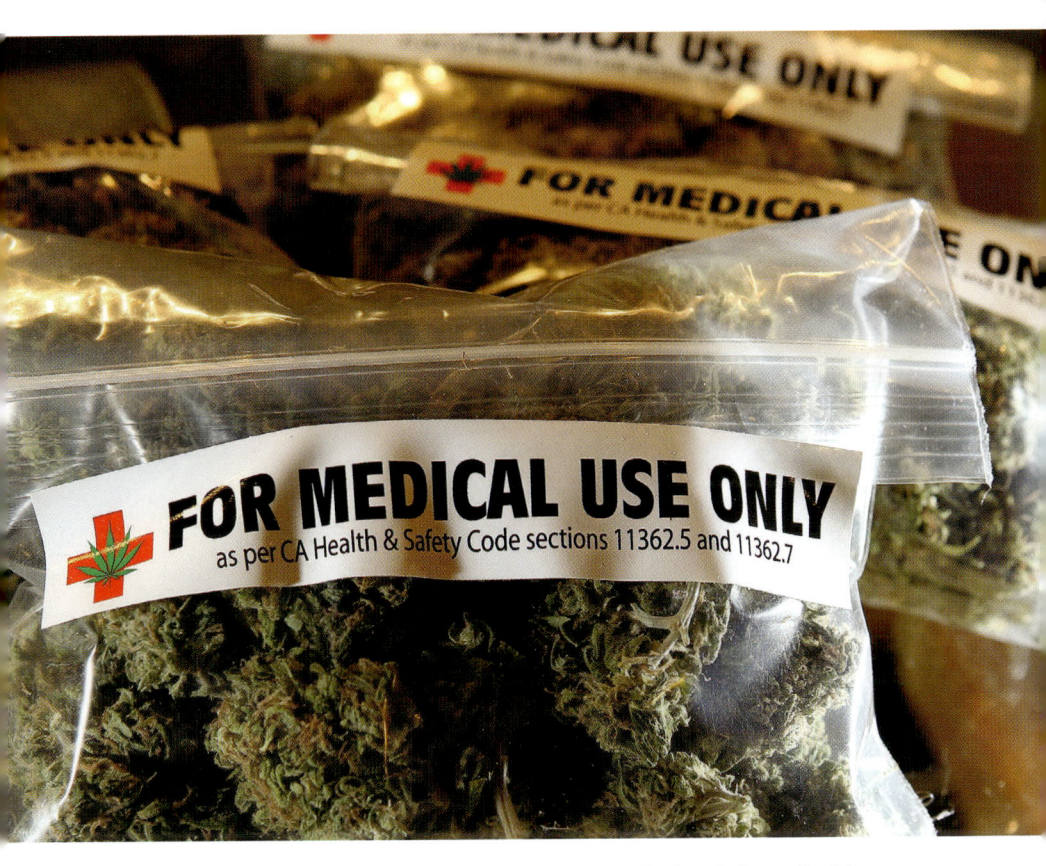

While many people say medical cannabis has helped them feel better, not everyone thinks it should be legal.

Advocates for medical cannabis were shocked and saddened by the Supreme Court decision. Angel Raich vowed to keep using cannabis. "It is absolutely cruel that the federal government does not allow us the right to use this medicine," Raich said. "It is not easy for us patients that really need this medicine … to have to fight for our lives on this kind of level."[9]

What's Next?

In recent years, more efforts have been made to attempt to repeal the prohibition on cannabis federally. However, as of early 2021, cannabis is still federally illegal in the United States. Some politicians are looking to change that, however. In February 2021, Senate Majority Leader Chuck Schumer, along with two other Democratic senators, said he planned to push to end the prohibition of cannabis on a federal level. Schumer, of New York, and Senators Cory Booker, of New Jersey, and Ron Wyden, of Oregon, released a statement, which specified it would also provide justice for those who had previously been convicted of cannabis-related crimes. The statement discussed how the "War on Drugs" has disproportionately targeted people of color. "Ending the federal marijuana prohibition is necessary to right the wrongs of this failed war and end decades of harm inflicted on communities of color across the country,"[10] the statement said. It continued, "But that alone is not enough. As states continue to legalize marijuana, we must also enact measures that will lift up people who were unfairly targeted in the War on Drugs."[11]

Even with recreational cannabis now legal in some states, it can still be difficult for people in many parts of the United States to get a prescription for medical cannabis. Of course, in the few states that have still not legalized it, it is impossible to get a legal prescription, even for people who have illnesses that would qualify them in the next state over. However, even in states with legalized medical cannabis, getting a prescription is not always easy. The list of conditions eligible for medical cannabis is often limited, and states often require doctors to have a special registration that allows them to prescribe the substance. In some areas, finding a registered doctor can be quite difficult. For this reason, people eligible for medical cannabis sometimes forego getting a prescription and continue to get the drug illegally in order to treat their ailments.

While medical cannabis has been legalized in many places across the United States and the world, there is still a long way to go to provide universal relief for those with conditions that could benefit from the drug. However, in the 2020 election, every item on the ballot that involved the decriminalization or legalization of the substance passed. For example, New Jersey and Arizona voters chose to legalize cannabis for adult recreational use, and Mississippi voters elected to legalize it for medical use. With state governments and senate officials leading the way, it may not be long before the federal government agrees to legalizing cannabis.

Your Opinion Matters!

1. Do you think the federal government should be able to prosecute cannabis-related crimes in states where the acts are legal?
2. Do you think medical cannabis should be limited to forms with low THC levels that won't get a user high?
3. Why do you think the federal government still hasn't legalized cannabis, even though many states have?

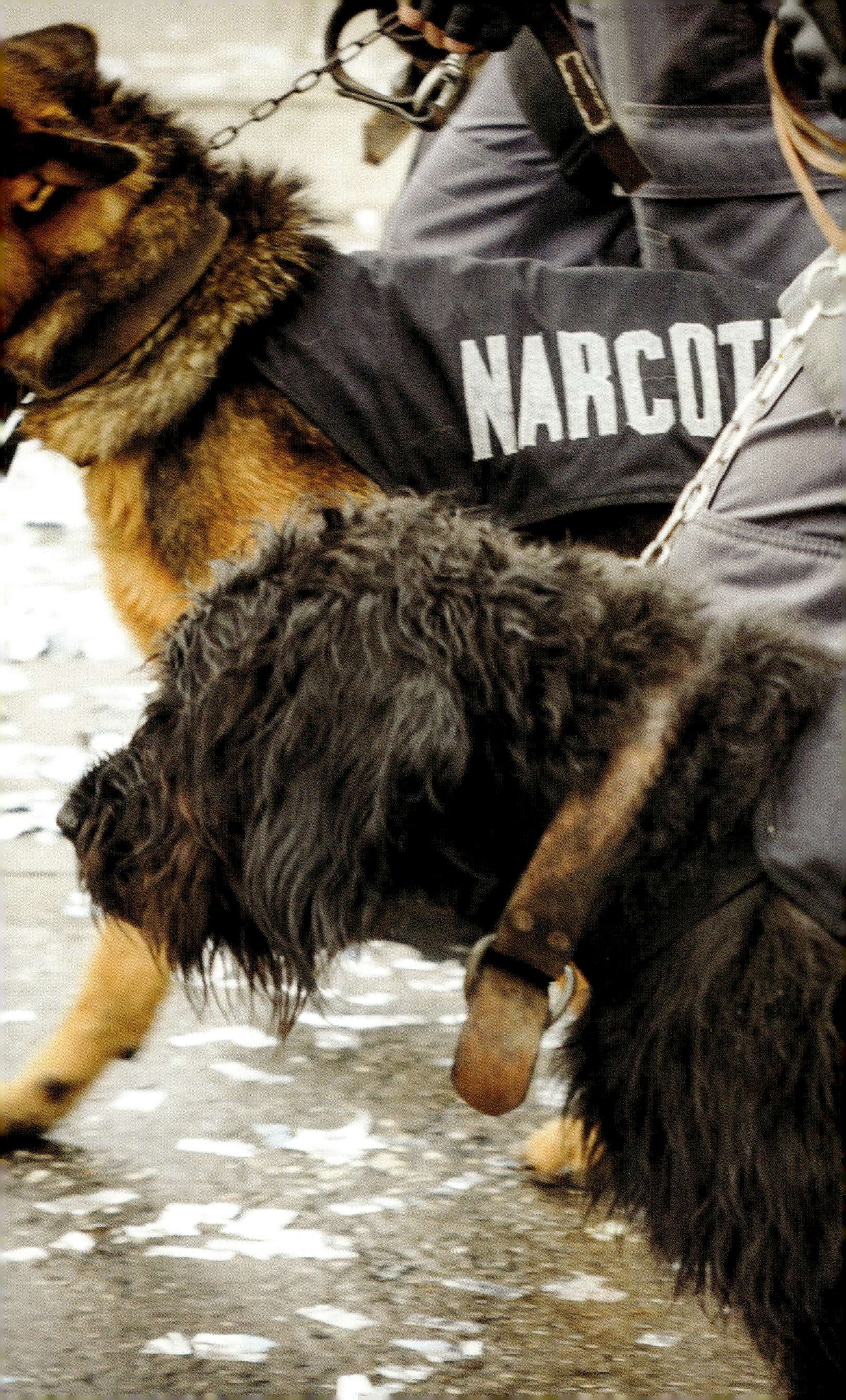
NARCOT

THE FUTURE OF LEGALIZATION

The fight for legal cannabis has been raging for as long as the substance has been banned. There are many reasons people believe the drug should be legal. In addition to medical and recreational reasons, many people feel that only legalization can fully fix the way nonviolent cannabis-related crimes are handled. Even in states where it has been decriminalized, there are still people in jail serving what many feel are harsh and unnecessary sentences.

As discussed earlier in this book, cannabis is still illegal at the federal level. When there is a disagreement between federal and state law, federal law wins. One thing this means is that, in addition to federal officials being able to charge people, even in states where cannabis is fully legal, there are also federal mandatory minimum laws in place. These laws say that a person who breaks that particular law must serve a minimum amount of time in jail and may even serve more. Judges have no ability to sentence less time for crimes that have a mandatory minimum penalty attached, but they can sentence more or impose a fine in addition to the jail sentence. For possession, the sentence is no less than 15 days in jail for a second offense and no less than 90 days for any subsequent offense, no matter how small an amount of cannabis

Narcotics dogs are specially trained dogs used by the police to sniff out illegal substances, including cannabis.

The Future of Legalization 73

the person is caught with. Many people believe these are unreasonably harsh penalties for a nonviolent crime, and some politicians have spoken out against mandatory minimums.

Another main argument presented by those in favor of legalization is that people should not be punished by the government for doing something that does not harm anyone except, arguably, themselves. People do things that have the potential to hurt themselves every day, but most of these things are not illegal unless they directly harm another person. For example, alcohol and tobacco are both legal even though they sometimes kill their users. However, drunk driving is not legal because it has the potential to kill or seriously injure innocent people. There are also laws regarding how close someone can stand to a building when he or she is smoking in order to prevent non-smokers from inadvertently inhaling secondhand smoke. For the same reason, most states also have laws about smoking indoors in public places.

Even with the growing support of legalization, there are still many who oppose it for all uses, as well as those who oppose it for recreational purposes but believe it should be legal only for medical purposes.

Legalization Pros

Studies show that the majority of Americans support legalizing cannabis. In addition to the 2019 survey from the Pew Research Center discussed in the introduction of this book, several other recent studies have shown similar results. Gallup has studied the public's view on legalization since 1969. That year, only 12 percent of Americans were reported to support it. However, Gallup has seen support for legalization change and grow over the years. By 1977, support had reached 28 percent. In following years, however, the rates dipped slightly. It wasn't until 2000 that support finally reached more than 30 percent. However, by 2020, that number had more than doubled, with 68 percent of American adults supporting cannabis legalization. Other data from Gallup reported that the same year, 70 percent of American adults thought smoking cannabis was morally acceptable. This was a leap of 5 percent in just one year.

According to a Gallup article by Megan Brenan:

> *The trajectory of the public's support for the legalization of marijuana has coincided with an increasing number of states approving it. It is not entirely clear whether the shift in public opinion has caused the change in many state laws or vice versa. Given recent trends, more states are likely to legalize recreational marijuana in the future. Considering the high level of public support for such a measure, a change in federal policy could even occur.*[1]

Many people have made the argument that cannabis is no more dangerous than alcohol or tobacco, both of which are legal for adults in the United States. The truth of such claims is difficult to determine because of differences in the substances and behavior of their users. Both cannabis and alcohol can have negative health effects if they are heavily used. However, there are many examples of people dying from drinking too much alcohol at one time but no such examples of people dying from smoking too much weed at one time. This leads some people to conclude that alcohol is more dangerous than weed, while others would say that is just one part of a much bigger equation. As for tobacco use, many of the same chemicals are present in both cigarettes and joints, but cannabis users tend to smoke less than cigarette users. Ultimately, more research is needed to determine whether any of these substances is more harmful than the others.

Regulating the distribution of cannabis has been recommended by some political leaders, who suggest that government control over cannabis is one way to keep gangs and drug lords out of the business. They point out that once alcohol was

While the merits and drawbacks of legalization for adults may be debatable, we know for sure that cannabis, like alcohol and tobacco, can be harmful to children, whose bodies are still growing and developing.

made illegal, the beer and liquor business was taken over by gangsters. When Prohibition was repealed, the gangsters were driven out of the business, and legal brewers and distillers took over. The same has proven true in cannabis legalization. The amount of weed being illegally imported from Mexico has drastically decreased in the last several years now that it is legal to grow it in parts of the United States. In places where it's legal, many people who formerly would have bought from a dealer now buy from a licensed dispensary, which can help support local or state economies.

Government regulation could also help ensure the purity of the drug. Pot that is not inspected may be carrying bacteria that could spread disease. Additionally, it is sometimes laced with other substances. This is generally done to bulk up the weight of the product so it can be sold for more money. In these cases, the buyer is not often aware of what has been added. Sometimes these substances are known to be harmful, but even if the substance the cannabis is being laced with is not generally harmful, it can become harmful if the unaware user is allergic to it. Other times, pot is laced with products to change the psychoactive effects. These combinations can be very dangerous, or even deadly.

If pot becomes legal nationally, federal agencies such as the Food and Drug Administration and the Department of Agriculture would be responsible for inspecting the crop and setting standards that would have to be followed for production. Also, U.S. border patrol agents would inspect cannabis as it arrives at the borders. Right now, of course, no illegal pot is inspected, and customers do not always know what they are inhaling. Scientific studies of cannabis plants have shown that they are sometimes contaminated with mold, *E. coli*, or pesticides.

When Prohibition was repealed in 1933, Congress quickly enacted a tax on alcohol that President Franklin Roosevelt used to finance the antipoverty programs of his New Deal that helped rescue Americans from the Great Depression. Since then, consumers of beer, wine, and liquor have continued to pay heavy taxes on the beverages. Supporters of legalizing cannabis suggest that if the government regulates the cannabis business, billions of dollars in new tax revenue could be raised. Most Americans would benefit because the other taxes they pay would be reduced. This has already happened in states where cannabis is legal recreationally.

In 2012, Colorado and Washington were the first states to legalize recreational cannabis. In the first year of legalization alone, Colorado sold $996,184,788 worth of pot and collected more than $135 million in taxes. In 2020, Colorado's annual revenue from cannabis sales was more than $2 billion. In November of that year, the state saw $32 million in taxes and fees brought in by cannabis sales.

Cannabis Around the World

While the United States is certainly making moves toward decriminalization and legalization of cannabis, these changes have largely only taken place over the past several years. In some other countries, people have long been given more freedom when it comes to cannabis. The trend started in Europe in 1990, when drug abuse experts from four European cities—Amsterdam in the Netherlands, Frankfurt and Hamburg in Germany, and Zurich in Switzerland—met in Frankfurt to discuss ways of fighting addiction. They concluded that the zeal to arrest, prosecute, and imprison drug offenders had not worked. The group of drug experts, who formed the organization European Cities on Drug Policy, found that most drug users are not criminals, and throwing them in jail exposes them to real criminals, making it more likely they would break laws when they are released from prison. The representatives at the Frankfurt conference suggested that it may be wiser to let people use soft drugs, such as pot and hallucinogenic

When cannabis is legalized, it becomes regulated, be it by local, state, or federal governments. This can help ensure that plants are not contaminated.

The Future of Legalization

What's NORML?

The National Organization for the Reform of Marijuana Laws (NORML) was founded in 1970 by R. Keith Stroup, a young lawyer who had worked for the United States National Commission on Product Safety, which was established to protect consumers from dangerous or faulty products. While working as a consumer advocate, he conceived of the idea of an organization to speak up for the rights of cannabis consumers.

In 1972, the National Commission on Marijuana, which had been appointed by President Richard Nixon, recommended that people who possess less than an ounce (28.3 g) of the drug should not be prosecuted. NORML brought the report to the attention of state legislatures, and due to NORML's efforts, five states—Alaska, California, Colorado, Maine, and Ohio—removed criminal penalties for possession of small amounts of the drug. According to NORML's website, Stroup "ran the organization through 1979, during which 11 states decriminalized minor marijuana offenses."[1]

NORML continues its work today. According to the group's website, its "mission is to move public opinion sufficiently to legalize the responsible use of marijuana by adults, and to serve as an advocate for consumers to assure they have access to high quality marijuana that is safe, convenient, and affordable."[2]

1. NORML.org, "R. Keith Stroup, JD," norml.org/about-norml/norml-board-of-directors/r-keith-stroup-j-d/ (accessed March 7, 2021).

2. NORML.org, "About NORML," norml.org/about (accessed March 7, 2021).

mushrooms, legally but to conduct public campaigns advising them of the risks and offering them programs to beat their addictions—much the same way alcohol and tobacco use is treated worldwide. However, they decided not to legalize hard drugs such as cocaine or heroin. They issued the Frankfurt Resolution, which states:

> Drug using is for the majority of users a temporary part of their biography, which can be overcome within the process

of maturing out of addiction. Drug policy may not render this process more difficult, but it must support this process ... A drug policy fighting against addiction exclusively with the criminal law and the compulsion to abstinence and offering abstinence only has failed ... Criminalization is a counterpart to drug aid and drug therapy and is a burden for police and justice they cannot carry ... The aid for drug users must no longer be threatened by criminal law ... It is necessary to lay stress on harm reduction and repressive forms of intervention must be reduced to the absolute necessary minimum.[2]

Since 1990, lawmakers in several European countries have adopted the spirit of the Frankfurt Resolution, particularly when it applies to cannabis use. In recent years, many European nations have legalized medical cannabis. Many more have decriminalized possession for any personal use in small amounts.

The Netherlands is regarded as having some of the most liberal pot rules in Europe. In the city of Amsterdam, sale and use of cannabis and hashish in public coffeehouses is permitted, although it cannot be used on the streets. However, this has become such a large draw for tourists that it has proven somewhat of a nuisance for locals. In early 2021, Amsterdam mayor Femke Halsema proposed a plan that would continue to allow cannabis products to be sold only to Dutch nationals and residents of the Netherlands. This would, in effect, end what has become known as "cannabis tourism" in Amsterdam.

Have the European countries that abide by the spirit of the Frankfurt Resolution seen their addiction rates decline, or has much of Europe simply turned into a safe harbor for cannabis users? There is dispute over the success of the Frankfurt Resolution. *The Huffington Post* reports that some Dutch citizens have complained about the legalization of cannabis, leading the government to reduce the number of legal coffeeshops in

This display in an Amsterdam coffee shop shows chocolates and other candy made with cannabis for sale.

the country. France and Germany have also complained; they share borders with the Netherlands and have seen an increase in the number of their citizens bringing pot into their countries, even though this is illegal. Some border towns tried to solve this problem by creating a registry for weed users, but "the independent-minded Dutch (especially young people), don't want to be registered as pot users, so they are buying it on the street—which is rekindling the black market, and will likely translate to more violence, turf wars, and hard drugs being sold."[3]

These problems aside, legalization has largely worked well for the Netherlands. Reports have shown that rates of Dutch people who use pot tend to be lower than those of Americans because it is treated as a mundane thing. By viewing cannabis as they do alcohol, some would say the Dutch have turned the problem from a criminal issue into a health issue.

Unfair Arrests

Typically, the DEA, the Federal Bureau of Investigation (FBI), and other federal law enforcement agencies do not target individual users of pot, especially since the substance has been decriminalized in so many places across the United States. Rather, federal agencies go after big-time drug lords. Still, penalties for simple possession are on the books, and individuals can be prosecuted in federal courts.

The 1986 mandatory minimum law was passed following the death of Len Bias, a college basketball star who celebrated his selection in the National Basketball Association (NBA) draft by going to a party and ingesting a fatal dose of cocaine. The nation was shocked by the death of Bias. Responding to intense public pressure, federal lawmakers felt compelled to come down hard on all drug offenders. Much to the dismay of legalization advocates, Congress included marijuana users on the list of offenders who could be prosecuted under the law.

What About Hemp?

Hemp is a form of cannabis, but it contains so little THC that getting high from it is impossible. Nevertheless, hemp was outlawed along with all other forms of cannabis in 1970 when the Controlled Substances Act said that cannabis had no legal purpose. Any hemp used legally for manufacturing in the United States was imported from other countries until 2014, when President Barack Obama exempted hemp from the Controlled Substances Act, making it legal to grow in the United States

Many types of rope are often made of hemp.

Legalization advocates insist that the 1986 law, as well as the many state laws that include jail sentences for offenders, has resulted in a tremendous number of people serving prison terms—both short and long—for cannabis offenses. Decriminalization and legalization has caused the total number of arrests to fall, but there is still a big inequality—Black and Latinx people are much more likely than white people to be

again. The move allowed for more research to be done and officially differentiated hemp from marijuana and recognized that it had legitimate uses not related to drug use. The Agricultural Improvement Act of 2018 aimed to expand on some aspects of the 2014 bill and officially removed hemp and hemp seeds from the DEA's list of controlled substances.

The seeds and stalks of the hemp plant have many uses, making hemp farming a profitable endeavor. For example, hemp oil extracted from the seed can be a component in fuel, lubricants, ink, varnish, paint, and cosmetics. The various parts of the stalk can create mulch, fiberboard, insulation, rope, clothes, cardboard, and ethanol. It is a sustainable crop that requires less water to grow than other crops, such as wheat, and can be used to purify soil, causing other crops to have fewer impurities.

President Barack Obama

arrested for the same crime, even though the usage rates are the same.

At least in theory, the legalization and decriminalization of cannabis should mean fewer people are sent to jail or prison for possession of the drug. This means jails and prisons should be less crowded and fewer tax dollars would be used to pay for prisoners' upkeep. However, in June 2020, it was estimated that around 40,000 Americans were still incarcerated for cannabis-related offenses, many in places where use of the drug has since been legalized.

According to the American Civil Liberties Union (ACLU), a group that works to defend individual rights and liberties guaranteed by the Constitution and laws of the United States, 88 percent of cannabis-related arrests between 2001 and 2010 were for simply possessing the drug. This means those people arrested were not charged with selling or intending to distribute the drug. Still, many of them ended up serving time in jail. In an analysis of data, the ACLU remarked, "Despite roughly equal usage rates, Blacks are 3.73 times more likely than whites to be arrested for marijuana."[4]

There are many complex reasons for why this happens. One is that police tend to concentrate their patrols in low-income areas, where more Black Americans are likely to live. Black Americans who are stopped by the police on the street or in a car may be asked to empty their pockets, regardless of whether they were doing anything illegal at the time. It is much rarer for police to ask a white person to do this, even if they were stopped for doing the same thing. If a person happens to illegally have cannabis in their possession when searched, they will likely be arrested and charged. So, if Black Americans are more likely to be searched, that also makes them more likely to be arrested. Many argue this is unfair and rooted in racism.

Unfortunately, there is no easy solution to the problem of racially disparate, or unequal, arrests. Some say that legalizing cannabis on the federal level could go a long way, but even that may not completely fix it, as people can still be arrested for things such as growing more plants than they are permitted or possessing more than the legally allowed amount. A massive overhaul of the way police departments function and the way our society views race is likely the only answer. In recent years, thanks to activists in the Black Lives Matter movement and other civil rights groups, some police

Racist arrests are a problem all across the United States. For years, people looking for change have protested, but unfortunately, the problem continues today.

The Future of Legalization 87

departments in the United States have begun to take steps toward change. However, much more still needs to happen in order to fully address these problems and make a widespread change to the system.

Looking Ahead

There are legitimate arguments on both sides of the cannabis legalization debate. However, as studies, as well as election results around the country, have shown, the majority of the people living in the United States are in favor of legalizing cannabis on some level. The majority of the country's states have legalized the substance for medical purposes. The number of states with legalized recreational pot is continuing to grow as well, and decriminalization is happening around the country. Those in favor of legalization for both purposes hope that the growing support from states will eventually prompt the federal government to legalize cannabis as well. Supporters often point to the time and money police could save if they did not have to arrest individuals who possessed small amounts of cannabis for personal use. They also state that cannabis is equally or even less harmful than alcohol and tobacco, and that the government has no business banning these items because it infringes on citizens' rights.

Still, many Americans are opposed to the legalization of cannabis completely. Opponents feel that cannabis is a dangerous, addictive drug with the potential to ruin lives and lead people to use harder drugs such as cocaine and heroin. Some recognize the benefits of medical cannabis and believe it should be legalized only for medicinal purposes. Others may recognize the benefits but are not in favor of legalizing it because they worry that it is a slippery slope toward recreational legalization. Still others sometimes claim that the health benefits are exaggerated or even fictionalized.

For a long time, there was a lack of scientific studies on cannabis and its effects. While there is still much more to be learned about the substance, it has become easier for researchers to obtain and perform tests on the drug, thanks to its legalization in certain states, thus expanding what we know about it. As more findings are published, public opinion may change, one way or another.

In addition to the general public's growing support, politicians and lawmakers have shown increased support for legalization in recent years. Many people believe it is only a matter of time before cannabis is legalized on the federal level in the United States. However, when it comes to cannabis, there is no way to know for sure what the future holds until it happens.

Your Opinion Matters!

1. Do you think there is a stronger argument for or against cannabis legalization for all purposes?
2. Do you agree with the main ideas behind the Frankfurt Resolution? Why or why not?
3. What is one thing you think police departments could do differently to change the racial inequality in cannabis-related arrests?

GETTING INVOLVED

The following are some suggestions for taking what you've just read and applying that information to your everyday life.

- Have a discussion with a trusted adult about their thoughts on cannabis legalization.

- Read more about both sides of the debate. Make sure the sources you're looking at are reliable!

- Remember, even if cannabis is legal where you live, it is still illegal (and harmful) for minors.

- Practice what you would say if a friend ever offered you cannabis.

- Never get in a car with a driver who is high—or under the influence of alcohol or other drugs.

NOTES

Introduction: Cannabis Culture
1. National Institute on Drug Abuse, "Most Commonly Used Addictive Drugs," July 2018, www.drugabuse.gov/publications/media-guide/most-commonly-used-addictive-drugs.

Chapter One: Cannabis Through Time
1. Drug Enforcement Administration, "Drug Scheduling," www.dea.gov/druginfo/ds.shtml.
2. Quoted in Edward M. Brecher, *Licit and Illicit Drugs* (Mount Vernon, NY: Consumers Union, 1972), p. 298.
3. Quoted in Larry Sloman, *Reefer Madness: A History of Marijuana* (New York, NY: St. Martin's Griffin, 1998), p. 48.
4. Quoted in Brecher, p. 411.
5. Dan Wakefield, *New York in the Fifties* (Boston, MA: Houghton Mifflin, 1992), p. 177.
6. Wakefield, p. 177.
7. Quoted in the *New York Times*, "Bethel Pilgrims Smoke 'Grass' and Some Take LSD to 'Groove,'" August 18, 1969, p. 25.
8. Quoted in the *New York Times*, "Bethel Pilgrims Smoke 'Grass' and Some Take LSD to 'Groove,'" p. 25.

Chapter Two: Cannabis's Impact on the Body
1. National Institute on Drug Abuse, "Marijuana Research Report: Is Marijuana Addictive?" July 2020, www.drugabuse.gov/publications/research-reports/marijuana/marijuana-addictive.
2. Quoted in Alvin Powell, "What We Know and Don't Know About Pot," *The Harvard Gazette*, February 24, 2020, news.harvard.edu/gazette/story/2020/02/professor-explores-marijuanas-safe-use-and-addiction/.
3. Quoted in Powell, "What We Know and Don't Know About Pot."
4. Quoted in Powell, "What We Know and Don't Know About Pot."

5. National Institute on Drug Abuse (NIDA), "Is Marijuana a Gateway Drug?" July 2020, www.drugabuse.gov/publications/research-reports/marijuana/marijuana-gateway-drug.

Chapter Three: Cannabis Today

1. Justice.gov, archived from National Drug Intelligence Center, "National Drug Threat Assessment 2005: Marijuana," www.justice.gov/archive/ndic/pubs11/12620/marijuana.htm.
2. Quoted in BBC News, "Sir Paul Reveals Beatles Drug Use," June 2, 2004, news.bbc.co.uk/1/hi/entertainment/music/3769511.stm.

Chapter Four: Medical Uses

1. Quoted in Brian Preston, *Pot Planet: Adventures in Global Marijuana Culture* (New York, NY: Grove, 2002), p. 255.
2. Quoted in Preston, p. 255.
3. Peter Grinspoon, MD, "Medical Marijuana," *Harvard Health Blog*, January 15, 2018, www.health.harvard.edu/blog/medical-marijuana-2018011513085
4. Quoted in *Consumer Reports*, "Marijuana as Medicine," May 1997, www.medmjscience.org/Pages/history/consumerreports.html.
5. Quoted in *Consumer Reports*, "Marijuana as Medicine."
6. Quoted in *Consumer Reports*, "Marijuana as Medicine."
7. Bailey Rahn, "6 Ways to Enjoy Cannabis without Having to Smoke It," Leafly, March 23, 2015, www.leafly.com/news/health/6-smoke-free-ways-to-consume-cannabis.
8. Quoted in Stephen Henderson, "Court Loss for Medical Marijuana," *Philadelphia Inquirer*, June 7, 2005, p. A-1.
9. Quoted in Erica Werner, "Medical Marijuana Advocates Implore Congress for Reform," Associated Press, *Santa Monica Daily Press*, May 5, 2005, backissues.smdp.com/050505.pdf.
10. Quoted in Christian Nunley, "Democratic Senators Will Push to Pass Pot Reform Bill this Year," CNBC, February 1, 2021, www.cnbc.com/2021/02/01/cannabis-reform-senators-say-they-will-push-pot-bill-in-2021.html.

11. Quoted in Nunley, "Democratic Senators Will Push to Pass Pot Reform Bill this Year."

Chapter Five: The Future of Legalization

1. Megan Brenan, "Support for Legal Marijuana Inches Up to New High of 68%," Gallup, November 9, 2020, news.gallup.com/poll/323582/support-legal-marijuana-inches-new-high.aspx.
2. Quoted in National Organization for the Reform of Marijuana Laws, "European Drug Policy," 2002, norml.org/index.cfm?Group_ID=4415#europe.
3. Rick Steves, "Amsterdam's Evolving Relationship with Weed," *Huffington Post*, August 1, 2012, www.huffingtonpost.com/rick-steves/the-latest-on-marijuana-l_b_1724763.html.
4. American Civil Liberties Union, "Marijuana Arrests by the Numbers," www.aclu.org/gallery/marijuana-arrests-numbers (accessed March 7, 2021).

FOR MORE INFORMATION

Books: Nonfiction

Giddens, Sandra. *Everything You Need to Know About the Risks of Marijuana*. New York, NY: Rosen Publishing, 2020.

Goldstein, Margaret J. *Legalizing Marijuana: Promises and Pitfalls*. Minneapolis, MN: Twenty-First Century Books, 2017.

New York Times Editorial Staff. *Marijuana*. New York, NY: New York Times Educational Publishing, 2019.

Books: Fiction

Duffy Stone, Heather. *Over the Tracks*. Minneapolis, MN: Darby Creek, 2015.

Kyi, Tanya Lloyd. *Prince of Pot*. Toronto, Ontario, Canada: Groundwood Books, 2017.

Neri, G. *Surf Mules*. Minneapolis, MN: Carolrhoda Lab, 2014.

Websites

Just the Facts!
www.youthnow.me/youth-teens/just-the-facts/
This educational page has information on many different drugs, including cannabis. It also has links to other informative resources.

Marijuana
kidshealth.org/en/teens/marijuana.html
This page offers more information about cannabis and the drug's effects. It also has a short section about what to do if you want to quit.

NIDA for Teens
teens.drugabuse.gov
Learn about the possible signs of a drug problem, complete activities, and learn more about many different types of drugs, including cannabis, on this website made specifically for teens. This website also includes informative videos and games.

Organizations

The American Civil Liberties Union (ACLU)
125 Broad Street
18th Floor
New York, NY 10004
www.aclu.org
instagram.com/aclu_nationwide
twitter.com/ACLU
youtube.com/ACLU
The ACLU fights to protect the individual rights and liberties guaranteed by the U.S. Constitution and laws to all people in the country. They're committed to fighting injustice and ensuring that individuals know the rights they have in important legal situations. The organization works in court and legislative systems, as well as directly in communities.

National Institute on Drug Abuse (NIDA)
3WFN MSC 6024
301 North Stonestreet Ave.
Bethesda, MD 20892
www.drugabuse.gov
twitter.com/NIDAnews
Part of the National Institutes of Health (NIH), NIDA's mission is to help move scientific study on the causes and impacts of drug use and addiction forward and to use the information found by such studies to improve public health, as well as individual health. NIDA's website offers plenty of information on cannabis use and abuse.

Substance Abuse and Mental Health Services Administration (SAMHSA)
5600 Fishers Lane
Rockville, MD 20857
National Helpline: 800-662-HELP (4357)
www.samhsa.gov
twitter.com/samhsagov
youtube.com/SAMHSA
Part of the U.S. Department of Health and Human Services, SAMHSA provides guidance for people who feel they need help with addiction or mental health. The organization aims to help lessen the impact of substance abuse and mental illness on people and communities in the United States. Heavy cannabis users who need help quitting can contact SAMHSA's national helpline or go on its website for information on addiction resources. The helpline is free, confidential, and available 24 hours. It provides information in both English and Spanish.

INDEX

A

Acosta, Pablo, 46, 48
acquired
  immunodeficiency
  syndrome (AIDS), 10, 53,
  57, 59, 61, 64, 67
addiction, 30–32, 78, 80–81
Agricultural Improvement Act
  of 2018, 85
Aispuro, Emma Coronel, 46
alcohol, 6, 15, 31, 50, 74–75,
  77, 80, 83, 88
Alzheimer's disease, 66
American Civil Liberties Union
  (ACLU), 86
American Medical
  Association (AMA), 53, 57,
  61
analgesic, 53, 61
anandamide, 30, 32
anesthetic, 9
Anslinger, Harry J., 16, 18
anxiety, 13, 38, 68
Arizona, 60, 64, 70
asthma, 34
attention deficit/
  hyperactivity disorder
  (ADHD), 66

B

Beat Generation, 18
bhang, 54
Bias, Len, 83
Booker, Cory, 70
border patrol agents, 44, 77
Burroughs, William S., 18
Bush, George H. W., 58

C

California, 14, 19, 45, 59–60,
  65, 80
Camarena, Enrique, 46
Canada, 7, 44–45
cancer, 5, 34, 53, 59, 61, 64,
  67
cannabidiol (CBD), 10, 12–13,
  38, 60, 65, 68
Cannabis indica, 10
Cannabis sativa, 10, 13, 18
cannabis use disorder (CUD),
  31
cartels, 45–46, 48
Centers for Disease Control
  and Prevention (CDC), 30
chemotherapy, 10, 53, 61, 64
China, 9
Chong, Tommy, 24

cocaine, 24, 30, 35, 37, 45–46, 48, 80, 83, 88
Colombia, 45–46
Colorado, 60, 78, 80
Compassionate Investigational New Drug program, 58
Congress, 13, 15–16, 24, 66, 77, 83
Constitution, 15, 86
Controlled Substances Act, 65, 67, 84–85
coordination, loss of, 32
Cyrus, Miley, 50

D

Davidson, Pete, 50
decriminalization, 6, 54, 59–61, 70, 73, 78, 80–81, 83–85, 88
dendrites, 28
Department of Agriculture, 77
depression, 9, 30, 68
dispensaries, 7, 37, 48, 77
dopamine, 27, 30, 37
Dr. Dre, 48
driving, 32–33
Drug Enforcement Administration (DEA), 10, 23, 46, 65, 83, 85
drug paraphernalia, 21–24, 48
drug smugglers, 44–45
drug test, 33
Dumas, Alexandre, 11

E

ecstasy, 11
Egyptian mummy, 9
18th Amendment, 15
epilepsy, 6
European Cities on Drug Policy, 78

F

Federal Bureau of Investigation (FBI), 83
Federal Bureau of Narcotics, 16, 18
Food and Drug Administration (FDA), 58, 77
Frankfurt Resolution, 80–81

G

Gallup, 74–75
gangsters, 15, 77
gateway drug, 35, 37
Ginsberg, Allen, 18
glaucoma, 6, 58–59, 61
gonorrhea, 9
government regulation, 77–78
Great Depression, 78
growers, 7, 43, 45, 65, 58, 67
Guthrie, Arlo, 21
Guzmán, Joaquín (El Chapo), 46, 48

Index **99**

H

Harrison Narcotic Act, 13
hashish, 10–11, 13–14, 81
head shops, 21–24, 38
hemp, 10–11, 13–14, 18, 84–85
heroin, 10, 35, 45–46, 48, 62, 80, 88
Hugo, Victor, 11

I

immigrants, 5
insomnia, 10, 57, 68

J

Jamaica, 44, 54

K

Kerouac, Jack, 18
K2, 38

L

Lady Gaga, 50
Latin America, 44
long-term effects of cannabis, 28
LSD, 10, 23, 38

M

Marihuana Tax Act, 16, 57
Marinol, 64
McCartney, Paul, 50
McConaughey, Matthew, 48
medical use of cannabis, 6–7, 10, 53, 57, 60, 64, 71
mental health, 68
methamphetamine, 24, 35, 38
Mexico, 7, 23, 44–46, 75
migraines, 57, 59
Mississippi, 58, 71
Monson, Diane, 65, 67–68

N

National Drug Intelligence Center, 44
National Highway Traffic Safety Administration, 33
National Institute on Drug Abuse (NIDA), 6, 37, 50, 62
National Organization for the Reform of Marijuana Laws (NORML), 80
Nation, Carry, 15
nausea, 5, 57, 64
Nelson, Willie, 48
Netherlands, 78, 81, 83
neurotransmitters, 28–31

O

Obama, Barack, 67, 84

100 The Marijuana Legalization Debate

obsessive-compulsive disorder (OCD), 66
ointment, 9
Operation Intercept, 23
Operation Pipe Dreams, 24

P

pain, 6, 9–10, 13, 53, 58, 61–62, 65
Parkinson's disease, 62
Pew Research Center, 7, 74
Phelps, Michael, 48
Polo, Marco, 11
Prohibition, 6, 15–16, 77
Proposition P, 15
Proposition 215, 15

Q

Quintero, Rafael Caro, 46, 48

R

Raich, Angel, 65, 67–69
Rastafarians, 54
receptors, 29
recreational purposes for cannabis, 6, 11, 14, 53, 60–62, 74
Reefer Madness, 17
religions, 54
resin, 10
Rogen, Seth, 50

S

Schedule I drugs, 10
Schumer, Chuck, 70
serotonin, 30
short-term effects of cannabis, 28
short-term memory, 6, 30
side effects of cannabis use, 14, 31–32, 61, 65
Sinaloa drug cartel, 46
Spice, 38
Stevens, John Paul, 67–68
Supreme Court, 66–67
synapses, 28
synthetic marijuana, 38

T

tetrahydrocannabinol (THC), 5, 9–10, 12–13, 27–28, 30, 32–33, 38, 60, 64–65, 68, 84
Thailand, 44
tinctures, 64–65
tobacco, 11, 23, 34, 74–75, 80, 88
Trump, Donald, 67
tunnels, 45

U

United States Department of Justice, 24, 65, 67
University of Mississippi, 58

V

vape pens, 51
Vietnam War, 19

W

Wakefield, Dan, 19–20

"War on Drugs," 70
Washington, George, 11
Woodstock Music and Art Fair, 19, 21
World War II, 18
Wyden, Ron, 70
Wyoming, 14

PHOTO CREDITS

Cover Canna Obscura/Shutterstock.com; p. 4 Anne-Marie Weber/Photolibrary/Getty Images Plus/Getty Images; p. 8 eldadcarin/iStock/Getty Images Plus/Getty Images; p. 12 Leon Neal/Staff/Getty Images News/Getty Images; p. 13 Smith Collection/Gado/Contributor/Archive Photos/Getty Images; p. 16 George Rinhart/Contributor/Corbis Historical/Getty Images; p. 17 Buyenlarge/Contributor/Archive Photos/Getty Images; p. 20 Evening Standard/Stringer/Hulton Archive/Getty Images; p. 22 Jeff Rotman/Photolibrary/Getty Images Plus/Getty Images; p. 26 Dmytro Tyshchenko/Shutterstock.com; p. 29 joshya/Shutterstock.com; p. 35 wildpixel/iStock/Getty Images Plus/Getty Images; p. 36 Steven D Starr/Contributor/Corbis Historical/Getty Images; p. 39 Spencer Platt/Staff/Getty Images News/Getty Images; p. 40 Vince Chandler/Contributor/Denver Post/Getty Images; p. 42 across/Shutterstock.com; p. 47 Octavio Hoyos/Shutterstock.com; p. 49 Noam Galai/Stringer/Getty Images Entertainment/Getty Images; p. 51 Todd Plitt/Contributor/Getty Images Entertainment/Getty Images; p. 52 Education Images/Contributor/Universal Images Group/Getty Images; p. 54 Pacific Press/Contributor/LightRocket/Getty Images; p. 56 Africa Studio/Shutterstock.com; p. 60 Kirill Vasikev/EyeEm/EyeEm/Getty Images; p. 63 Mendocino Coast Films/Moment/Getty Images; pp. 66, 69 Justin Sullivan/Staff/Getty Images News/Getty Images; p. 72 Andres Ruffo/EyeEm/EyeEm/Getty Images; p. 76 John Sommer/E+/Getty Images; p. 79 Bloomberg/Contributor/Bloomberg/Getty Images; p. 82 Laszlo Szirtesi/Contributor/Getty Images News/Getty Images; p. 84 ullstein bild/Contributor/ullstein bild/Getty Images; p. 85 Europa Press News/Contributor/Europa Press/Getty Images; p. 87 Andrew Burton/Staff/Getty Images News/Getty Images.

ABOUT THE AUTHOR

Kate Mikoley is a writer and editor living in Sloan, New York. Prior to her start in children's publishing, she worked as a journalist in Upstate New York, reporting on community events and politics. In her spare time, she enjoys hiking, jogging, knitting, and attempting (sometimes successfully) to restore old furniture.